Better Together

Kirk House Publishers

Better Together

CELEBRATING SERVICE DOG TEAMS

SUSAN AUNE

Better Together: Celebrating Service Dog Teams
Copyright © 2022 by Susan Aune

First Edition
Paperback-978-1-952976-52-0
Ebook-978-1-952976-53-7
Hardcover-978-1-952976-54-4
Library of Congress Control Number: 2022906121

Ghost Writer: Jett Sophia
Cover and Interior Design by Ann Aubitz
Photos by Susan Aune unless otherwise noted
Back cover photo: Rod Baakkonen

Published by Kirk House Publishers
1250 E 115th Street
Burnsville, MN 55337
Kirkhousepublishers.com
612-781-2815

Foreword

I spent almost thirty-five years working in the assistance dog industry, and it never ceases to amaze me how the lives of people with disabilities are improved by their assistance dogs. These individuals, whose lives are so powerfully impacted by one or more disabilities, are often uplifted and renewed when a talented and loving canine partner enters their life.

One of my favorite opportunities as executive director at Can Do Canines was to attend the live graduation ceremonies that occur a few times each year at our facility. Getting to spend a few minutes with each of the graduates, to hear about how their lives had been improved by their assistance dog, motivated me to train even more dogs for those who were still on our waiting list.

Susan's stories offer us a peek into the lives of people with a variety of disabilities, all at different points in their relationship with an assistance dog. This intimate, behind-the-scenes look at the impact of these special helpers provides a look into their lives that I was never able to see at those graduation events. In fact, reading these stories myself provided special and unexpected insights for me, even though I have known some of these people personally.

Most readers of this book have pets and truly love them. Reading this book helps us understand the contrast between a pet and an assistance dog and how intense these special, interdependent relationships are.

~Alan M. Peters
Can Do Canines Founder

Preface

L andscapes and flowers are usually my choice of subjects to photograph, but I was inspired to create this book one sunny summer day in 2019 when I witnessed an interaction between an assistance dog and her people. The location was a local garden park and there was a music festival. A couple was singing along with the music to their assistance dog. I knew instantly that the incredible bond I witnessed that summer day between a dog and her humans was very special. In a world where darkness can and does exist, I felt compelled to share the light and love of that moment.

That was my inspiration.

Later I realized that in my moment of observation with the couple and their dog, I had recognized only their ability to love, not their disabilities.

Meeting the assistance dog teams in this book solidified my desire to expand the goal for the book to include sharing the side of people with disabilities that we all can relate to—not just as dog lovers or people with struggles but as gardeners, campers, adventurers, writers, and leaders who are kind, funny, creative, and giving, to name but a few traits. I came to realize the teams were ordinary people living with extraordinary circumstances and doing so with a grace I am not sure I would have if I were in their situations. As a result, I have been able to confront some of my own prejudices about people with disabilities, and feel I have grown as a human.

The human team members I met are impressively good dog trainers! I have trained dogs for agility, obedience, and scent work, so I know the diligence it takes to make a dog succeed happily and well at a task. Certainly obedience and sometimes scent work are parts of assistance dog training, but assistance dogs are the superheroes of dog work, going above and beyond sport dog training. Sometimes they even train themselves! They need their people to keep their training ongoing and consistent so they can be the best assistance dogs they can be.

I was excited to meet some teams, do some interviews, and take pictures. Unexpectedly, finding teams to interview proved to be a challenge, due to federal health privacy laws that restricted agencies from giving me any information about assistance dog teams to contact.

Like my serendipitous first team at the garden park, the next team I found was through happenstance—at a home improvement store. From then on I asked everyone I knew if they knew of any assistance dog teams. This approach garnered me a few more teams. Then came my contact with the Can Do Canines director—now retired—Alan Peters, who was so welcoming to me. Ultimately, although I approached many additional organizations, Can Do Canines provided the best avenue for assistance dog teams to contact me without violating any privacy laws; therefore, Can Do Canine teams are heavily represented in the book. While I may have taken a slight editorial liberty here and there, the stories are true as told to me.

During the making of this book, the COVID-19 pandemic arrived and shut down person-to-person contact for about a year. Meanwhile, I was learning and growing as a photographer, moving on from flowers to learning how to photograph dogs and people. In 2021, when restrictions lifted, I was ready to go on the road, all over Minnesota, for more interviews. Things are gradually opening up now from the COVID-19 pandemic, and I look forward to connecting with the friends I have made on this journey. It is an honor to tell the teams' stories, and I hope I do them justice. This is their book as much as mine.

Contents

Introduction

For this book, my goal is to share images and stories that capture the loving bond between assistance dogs and their people. My hope is that you will get to know the people and dogs presented here and come to like them as much as I have. Before you meet them though, I have included some important background information about assistance dogs. This information will answer many questions that might arise while reading the stories.

Assistance dog or service dog—what is the difference? The term assistance dog is used for dogs helping people with disabilities, while service dogs, a more general term, also can include military and police dogs. The Americans with Disabilities Act (ADA),[1] a federal law, uses the term *service animal* for dogs (and some miniature horses) trained to help people with disabilities, while agencies who train dogs for people with disabilities most often use the term *assistance dog*. In this book, I will use the term assistance dog except when talking about the ADA or when quoting a team member.

Can Do Canines, a nonprofit assistance-dog training organization in Minnesota, capitalizes and uses the terms Mobility Assist Dog, Diabetes Assist Dog, Hearing Assist Dog, Seizure Assist Dog, and Autism Assist Dog.

There are many types of assistance dogs, and not all are represented in this book. The people in this book volunteered to participate.

There is no medical advice in this book. If you have a medical condition, please consult your medical professional.

When I began this journey almost three years ago, I knew nothing about assistance dogs. Reading about service animals in the Americans with Disabilities Act was a good place to start learning about them. The movie *Crip Camp: A Disability Revolution* (2020)[2] is a fascinating history of how the ADA came about. It can be viewed on Netflix and is also available on YouTube on the internet.

The ADA defines service dogs "as dogs that are individually trained to do work or perform tasks for people with disabilities. The work or task a dog has been trained to provide must be directly related to the person's disability. Dogs whose sole function is to provide comfort or emotional support do not qualify as service animals under the ADA."[3] For this book, I have only included dogs who meet the ADA definition of a service dog. Importantly, the

ADA does not certify service dogs, and there is no national certification program for service or assistance dogs. There is no requirement that a dog wear a vest while working, but many do so.

Assistance dogs are working dogs. When working, assistance dogs are to be considered a medical aid and are not to be spoken to or touched by the public, any more than you would touch someone's wheelchair or cane. So if you see an assistance dog team, please do not approach to pet or talk to the dog. If you feel you must approach, please speak with the handler before doing anything with the dog. Be prepared—they may not allow you to interact with their dog.

Since there is no federal assistance dog certification or list of training requirements beyond being trained to do a task specific to a person's disability, the International Association of Assistance Dog Partners (IAADP) provides some parameters for training. The following standards are paraphrased from the IAADP Minimum Training Standards for Public Access.[4]

IAADP has standards for assistance dogs in public places. Here are the requirements:

1. Hours of training: At least 120 hours of training, including homework, with at least 30 of those hours in public places. Agencies who use the IAADP standards and certify their own dogs may require a log verifying hours of training. A sample training log is available on the IAADP website.

2. Obedience: Dogs must consistently obey "sit, stay, come, down, and heel" as well as reliably come to handler, in public, if the leash is dropped and handler says or signs "come".

3. Manners: A well-behaved dog means:
    *   No aggression towards other people or dogs
    *   No begging for food or for petting while working
    *   No sniffing objects, dogs, or people while working
    *   No grabbing food or objects off the floor or shelves unless handler dropped the object
    *   No pulling on the leash, lunging, barking or growling
    *   No urinating or defecating in public unless indicated in a designated area

4. Tasks: Assistance dogs are trained to do specific tasks to help their handler, such as pick up

dropped items or alert to sounds or medical conditions. The IAADP website has more detail on what a task is or is not.

5. Prohibited: Any aggressive or attack-trained dogs. Any training that encourages aggression.

6. Trainer/Handler responsibilities: Trainers can be a person with a disability, staff of an assistance dog training agency, a volunteer who is training dogs or puppies, or the loved one of a person with a disability who is assisting with training. Trainers are responsible for:

- Ensuring the dog is clean, healthy, vaccinated, and free of parasites
- Respecting other people and property
- Using positive (reward based) training methods
- Monitoring dog while working so it is not over-stressed
- Immediately cleaning up any dog messes (carry bags and paper towels)
- Willingly and politely educating the public about assistance dogs and the laws about them.

Trainers represent the entire assistance dog community so always need to be on their best behavior.

For further information, please consult the IAADP website at: https://iaadp.org.

Assistance dogs can be trained by an individual or an organization. There are some of each included in this book. Beginning references for someone interested in training their own dog are the *Teamwork I* [5] and *Teamwork II* [6] books by Stuart Nordensson. The tasks assistance dogs are trained to do must be specific to the person's disability and need, so each partnership must be individualized. Training from start to finish for a dog can take two years or more and takes a team of people. Assistance dogs must be under control at all times and in all situations. They are models of good dog behavior.

Some assistance dog agencies breed their own dogs for health and trainability; some use rescue, shelter, or donated dogs. After a dog is selected, there may be puppy raisers, socializers, and then final trainers. Dogs are often about two years old when ready to be paired with a person with a disability. In other words, it can take about two years to train a service dog.

The agencies that train assistance dog teams are not required to be licensed or standardized. An international organization, Assistance Dogs International (ADI), provides standards for charitable assistance dog training agencies. In this book, I only refer to agencies that are ADI-accredited, as that allows for some standardization and high standards of training. Not all assistance dog agencies train all types of assistance dogs, so the ADI has a list of their certified agencies and what types of assistance dogs the agency trains. This is useful for someone looking for a trained assistance dog.

Each assistance dog training agency also determines their requirements for applications and fees for those seeking an assistance dog. The types of service dogs that ADI nonprofit or charitable organizations train are mobility service dogs, post-traumatic stress disorder (PTSD) veteran's service dogs, autism service dogs, diabetic alert service dogs, seizure service dogs, psychiatric service dogs, and medical alert service dogs, as well as hearing dogs and guide dogs. Again, an agency may focus on training just a few types of assistance dogs. In 2018 (the most current statistics on the ADI website), the total number of all types of assistance dogs placed by ADI-certified organizations was 16,766 worldwide, with 2,864 of those being new assistance dog teams in the North America and Oceania regional chapters.[7] There is an ongoing shortage of assistance dogs.

According to the Centers for Disease Control and Prevention (CDC), in the United States, one in four adults (61 million people) live with a disability. The CDC delineates these six functional disability types: mobility, cognition, independent living, hearing impaired or deaf, vision loss, and self-care. Not surprisingly, adults with disabilities are up to five times more likely than people without disabilities to experience mental distress. Studies have found that adults with disabilities are more likely to have other health concerns related to frequent mental distress than adults without disabilities, such as depressive disorders and a lack of access to healthcare.[8,9]

The good news is that service dogs can alleviate "strain, increase independence, and decrease the risk of social isolation," which all contribute to improvements in mental health as well as physical health.[10] A good story of how a service dog can positively impact a person's life and family is *Endal: How One Extraordinary Dog Brought a Family Back from the Brink* (Parton, 2009).[11]

The bad news is that due to the high cost of raising and training a service dog (from 25 to 50 thousand dollars), as well as a high failure rate of dogs in training (50–70 percent), wait times for a service dog can vary from months to years.[12]

The shortage of assistance dogs was recently mentioned in an article in the *Minneapolis StarTribune*.[13] As assistance dog's roles have expanded, the demand for them has increased. Meanwhile, the lack of regulations in certification and training of assistance dogs nationally is leading to higher prices and a risk of poor service from some unaccredited assistance-dog trainers. People who are considering getting an assistance dog need to proceed with caution.

All of the people I interviewed agreed that assistance dogs are of great benefit to a person with a disability, so if you are looking for an assistance dog, be cautious but not deterred. I hope this introduction gives you some good places to start your search, particularly with information from Assistance Dogs International.

The teams are not presented in any particular order other than the first one and the last one.

Now let us learn what life is like with an assistance dog.

References

1. "Service Animals," ADA.gov, https://www.ada.gov/service_animals_2010.htm.
2. *Crip Camp: A Disability Revolution.* Directed by Nicole Newnham and James Lebrecht. Good Gravy Films and Higher Ground Productions, 2020. https://www.netflix.com/title/81001496
3. https://www.ada.gov/
4. "Minimum Training Standards for Public Access." International Association of Assistance Dog Partners, accessed May 5, 2022, https://www.iaadp.org/iaadp-minimum-training-standards-for-public-access.html
5. Stewart Nordensson and Lydia Kelley, *Teamwork: A Dog Training Manual for People with Disabilities, Book One: Basic Obedience* (Tucson: TOP DOG Publications, 1997).
6. Stewart Nordensson and Lydia Kelley, *Teamwork II: A Dog Training Manual for People with Disabilities, Book Two: Service Exercises* (Phoenix: Happy Tails Service Dogs, 2010).
7. "Member Program Statistics," Assistance Dogs International, accessed March 2, 2022, https://assistancedogsinternational.org/members/member-program-statistics/.

8. "Disability Impacts All of Us," Centers for Disease Control and Prevention, accessed March 2, 2022. https://www.cdc.gov/ncbddd/disabilityandhealth/infographic-disability-impactsall.html

9. "Frequent Mental Distress Among Adults with Disabilities: An Easy-Read Summary," Centers for Disease Control and Prevention, accessed March 2, 2022, https://www.cdc.gov/ncbddd/disabilityandhealth/easy-read-frequent-mental-distress.html.

10. Martina Lundqvist, Lars-Åke Levin, Kerstin Roback, and Jenny Alwin, "The Impact of Service and Hearing Dogs on Health-Related Quality of Life and Activity Level: A Swedish Longitudinal Intervention Study," *PubMed*, accessed March 2, 2022, https://www.pubmed.ncbi.nim.nih.gov/29945630.

11. Allen Parton and Sandra Parton, Endal: How One Extraor*dinary Dog Brought a Family Back from the Brink* (London: Harper Collins Publishers, 2009).

12. "Service Dogs 101: Everything You Need to Know about Service Dogs," American Kennel Club, accessed March 2, 2022, https://www.akc.org/expert-advice/training/service-dog-training-101/ .

13. Markian Hawryluk, "The Bite of a Service Dog Shortage," *Minneapolis Star Tribune*, March 6, 2022, section 5H, p. 2.

The Teams

"A hero is an ordinary individual who finds the strength to persevere and endure in spite of overwhelming obstacles."
~Christopher Reeve

The picture that launched a book.

Chapter 1

TRACEY, KEITH, and MAYA

*"Maya has been with us through a lot
of trauma and challenges, and that has created a special bond
and a deep level of trust."*

I first met Tracey and Keith by chance at a lovely garden park, which coincidentally is where they first met each other twenty-five years ago. Maya, a beautiful black Labrador retriever mix, was with them, as she always is. I knew enough not to reach out to pet Maya, or even to look at her, but it was hard to resist.

The following week, I met with Tracey and Keith at Tracey's apartment courtyard. Tracey is a writer, and her favorite author is Maya Angelou. Keith is a longtime civil rights activist, so Maya Angelou was important in his life, too. Maya Angelou's death was a loss for them both. They got their new dog shortly after she died, and knowing that the dog would be tremendously important in both of their lives, providing mobility assistance, they named her Maya. Maya's been with them now for three years and was a rescue dog. Before Maya, there was Buddy.

Twenty years ago, Tracey had just had her fifth back surgery and she was mostly confined to bed. Keith was uneasy when he had to leave the apartment. *What if she dropped something she needs?* he thought. *She won't be able to pick it up.* There were a lot of things she would not be able to do, yet Keith had to leave from time to time. This was when they started thinking about getting an assistance dog.

Keith had grown up with dogs, often more than one at a time, but Tracey's only real experience with a dog had been a traumatic one. She was with her little brother when he was attacked by a black Labrador. After that, she was terrified of big dogs, especially black Labradors. So when Keith suggested a service dog, she agreed, but with one condition—it could not be a big dog. She thought a cute little terrier would be just right as a service dog for her.

Keith knew a woman who rescued dogs, so he called her and asked her to keep them in mind if she came across a dog she thought would be a good assistance dog. Two weeks later, the woman called back and said she'd found the dog she thought would be perfect for them—a big, beautiful dog, part black Labrador and part Newfoundland—a very big, very black dog. She asked when she could bring the dog by for them to meet him.

"No," said Tracey, "Absolutely not, she cannot bring that dog here." The rescue woman persisted, "I really think he could be the right one." Keith thought they could at least take a look at the dog, and although Tracey was reluctant, she finally relented. When the day arrived that they were to meet the dog, Tracey was nervous and fearful. Then came the knock on the door; her heart began beating so fast, too fast, and she wasn't sure she could go through with it. Keith opened the door, and without even giving Keith a glance, the big black dog trotted into the room and made a beeline for Tracey. He sat down next to her, put his head in her lap, and gazed up at her with his big brown eyes. Tracey's heart melted. They called him Buddy.

Buddy's photo courtesy of Keith

Then they got to work.

Because of Keith's extensive experience with dogs, they had chosen not to get an assistance dog through an agency, but to train one by themselves. While Keith had trained dogs in the past, he had never trained one to be an assistance dog, so in order to train, they also had to learn. For the next two years, assistance dog training was their number one focus twenty-four hours a day, seven days a week.

First they took Buddy through two levels of obedience training to get the basics down. They thought, *We can build on that*. Assistance dog training goes way beyond obedience, so they read and watched everything they could find that was specifically about training assistance dogs. Two books were especially helpful—*Teamwork*[1] and *Teamwork II*[2]—manuals specifically for people with disabilities who want to train their own assistance dogs using positive training methods (reinforcing behavior you want with treats rather than punishing behavior you do not want).

Training your own assistance dog is a constant effort, where every moment is a teachable moment. Training never really stops; it's refreshed during the entire life of the relationship. There is no doubt the first two years were the most intense—there was so much for both the dog and the humans to learn! Fortunately, Buddy was an eager leaner, and Tracey and Keith were eager learners, too.

One thing they learned is that you have to break complicated tasks down to smaller steps, for example, retrieving dropped objects. Keith explains, "When you start throwing a ball, they're likely to run in the other direction! Eventually, they decide to bring it back to you. Once they get good at that, you throw it less distance and less distance, until you can finally drop it right in front of you and they pick it up give it to you."

Keith and Tracey also use hand signals with their dogs. At the beginning with Buddy, they were using hand signals unconsciously—at the same time as they spoke the cue word, they'd naturally gesture. Strangely enough, they noticed that Buddy did what they asked before they even uttered a word—because they had started the command with a gesture! Buddy had learned the hand signal, even though they hadn't purposefully taught it to him. It was as though Buddy had taught them how to use hand signals and now Maya had learned hand signals too.

Keith says that he can't emphasize enough that training your own assistance dog is challenging and time-consuming work. It is also great fun, joyful, and creates a special, close relationship with the dog. They tell me that the bond they had with Buddy, and that they now have with Maya, is different from the bond between a person and a pet dog. Assistance dogs and their people share a deep and profound trust.

Maya

I wondered if it was easier to train Maya, with them already having trained Buddy. They both said it was easier in the sense that they did not have to do so much intensive learning themselves, but the dog training was no less rigorous. Again, they were lucky that Maya loved learning, just as Buddy had. They acknowledged that training your own assistance dog is not for everyone, since it is a long process of daily attention to every detail. Although it may be hard work, it is highly rewarding work. Another rewarding thought is since they trained their own dogs, agency-trained dogs were available for other people with disabilities. Win, win.

As assistance dog handlers, it was not just dog training skills that Keith and Tracey needed to learn. When they first got Buddy, their landlord said he was too big and they could not have him in their apartment. They researched the law, studied federal and state regulations relating to service animals, and learned that their landlord could not specify the size of their dog since he was a service dog. They kept Buddy and they became local experts on the law and on assistance dog training. Now other people turn to them for guidance.

Legally, assistance dogs can go anywhere with their handlers. Keith says getting a dog ready to "go anywhere" is a gradual training process: "You don't start out by taking the dog into a store with narrow aisles and breakable objects!" You start out in large, enclosed spaces with few distractions, and ever so gradually, the spaces get smaller and the distractions more numerous, until finally you can take your assistance dog anywhere. When Tracey was in the hospital for an extended stay, Keith and Buddy both stayed in the room with her. Buddy was welcomed because he was so well-behaved.

Buddy once flew with Tracey and Keith to New York City. Due to Buddy's size (110 pounds!) the airline upgraded them to first class and seated them in the front row, where there was a bit more legroom. Buddy stayed "on a down" at their feet for the entire three-hour flight. At the end of the flight, when the tires touched down, he sat up. People around them exclaimed in surprise—they had not even known there was a dog onboard!

As soon as they knew they would be flying to New York with Buddy, training started. On the internet they found sound recordings of airplanes taking off and landing. They played those for Buddy so he wouldn't be taken by surprise by the noise of the airplane. Plan ahead, they say, prepare yourselves and your dog, and things will go smoothly. The effort of all the extra training will pay off.

Along with being well-trained, an assistance dog has to be in excellent physical condition because it has to be on duty every day. The veterinarian (vet) is an important member of the team. Like everything else, a visit to the vet requires training. Keith says, "One thing we do is visit the vet when we don't have an appointment. Let [Maya] sniff around the parking lot and the building, and give her a treat. Let the vet techs and receptionist make a fuss over her. Let them give her a treat. Let the veterinarian greet her and give her a treat. Make it a fun outing. Then go home without having to have any kind of medical procedure. That way, when we have to go in for a shot or some other treatment, instead of being afraid of the vet's office, she's happy to go there. Take your dog to the vet when you're not taking your dog to the vet!" Good advice for all dogs, not just service dogs.

One time, Tracey and Keith were both in the hospital for what they thought would be a couple of days. Buddy was to be boarded at their veterinarian's clinic. Keith had complications, which turned several days into a six-week stay. The veterinarian told them to not worry as they would take good care of Buddy. And they did—the staff took him out for walks, played with him, and did Buddy's favorite thing—they scratched his belly! Gratefully, they only charged a nominal fee for their exceptional services. A good relationship with your veterinary clinic is essential.

Keith and Tracey had Buddy for thirteen years before Buddy got cancer and finally had to be euthanized. The veterinarian kindly came to their home to do it, and several people from the building came to say goodbye to Buddy. He was loved by many, many people—a "one in a million" dog, says Keith.

Keith and Tracey haven't flown with Maya yet, but she goes everywhere with them, and Tracey and Keith are definitely people on the go. They travel all around town, including on some very busy and loud streets, but Maya has been trained to not be upset or distracted by the noise. Of course, Keith says, you don't start by walking on the busiest street in town! You start small, by walking on relatively quiet side streets, and gradually go to busier and busier streets. Maya now can walk anywhere with Keith without getting ruffled. They are often seen around town.

Assistance dogs have to learn to do things that do not come naturally to them. For example, Tracey is terrified of thunderstorms, and one of Buddy's jobs was to comfort Tracey when she was anxious—but thunderstorms made him anxious too! He had to overcome his own anxiety in order to help Tracey. He would hear thunder and then run straight to Tracey. They would hold each other until the storm was over; it is not just physical tasks that assistance dogs are able to help with!

Maya has also learned to comfort Tracey when Tracey becomes anxious. One thing Tracey does when she is anxious is rub her head. Maya knows that is a cue to get close to Tracey, so Tracey can rub her hands through Maya's fur instead—an action that soothes and calms both of them.

Here is another example of emotional connection and support. There is a movie that Tracey and Keith enjoy watching although Tracey always cries at one scene. The movie is a musical, and when the song that accompanies the sad scene starts, Maya immediately goes to sit close to Tracey and leans against her, as if to say "You don't have to be sad alone. I'm here with you."

There came a time when Tracey needed a greater level of nursing care than was available where they were living, so she moved to an assisted-living facility. Keith still lives in their old apartment with Maya, and most days, he and Maya make the five-mile trek to be with Tracey. It's hardest in the winter, of course, but they are a team, the three of them, and they need to be together as much as possible. Maya is a good bus traveler if she needs to go on the bus with Keith.

As Keith goes out and about with Maya, he finds that he has become a people trainer as well.

Many people have no idea how to interact with an assistance dog. Basically, Keith says, you do not interact with the dog—you do not look at it, do not speak to it, do not reach out to it—do not acknowledge it in any way. You interact with the handler, not the dog. Make eye contact with the handler, not the dog. Speak to the handler, not the dog. And remember that all handlers are different. One handler might be okay with you petting the dog, while another will never, ever allow it. Always ask. Even if one time a handler told you it was okay to talk to the dog, it does not mean it will be okay the next time. Always ask the handler before interacting with an assistance dog.

Tracey and Keith actually trained Buddy in a different language, so other people would not be able to interfere by trying to give him cues. Tracey and Keith were studying Ojibwe at the time, and many of Buddy's cues were in Ojibwe!

If you have asked, and if the handler has said you can speak to the dog, do not do anything until the hander has given the dog the off-duty cue. Keith demonstrates. We have been sitting outside with Maya lying quietly by Keith, not interacting in the conversation at all, although she is clearly watching both Keith and Tracey. She pays absolutely no attention to this interviewer. Then Keith sings out, *"Maya, quitting time!"* and immediately Maya is a different dog! She sits up, looks around, wags her tail, and then trots around the room with a greeting for each of us, me included.

Keith says, "Ninety percent of dog training is people training. Granted I made up that statistic, but that's what it feels like sometimes."

Tracey quips, "Ninety percent of statistics are made up on the spot!" Even Maya seems to be laughing.

References

1. Stewart Nordensson and Lydia Kelley, *Teamwork: A Dog Training Manual for People with Disabilities, Book One: Basic Obedience* (Tucson: TOP DOG Publications, 1997).

2. Stewart Nordensson and Lydia Kelley, *Teamwork II: A Dog Training Manual for People with Disabilities, Book Two: Service Exercises* (Phoenix: Happy Tails Service Dogs, 2010).

Chapter 2

JACOB and RAVEN

*"A service dog can bring
a vast improvement to your life."*

Jacob, who has a vision impairment, and Raven, a guide dog, are both young—Jacob is eighteen and Raven is not yet two—and they have been together for only nine months. As young and inexperienced as they both are, they are already a formidable team.

Jacob is attending a university, his first semester. You could say that Raven is in her first semester too—as a working guide dog. Together they do some remarkable things. Here is one example: Jacob will say *"find biology class,"* and off they go, with Raven confidently and happily leading the way to the biology classroom. They make it look easy. There was one time when a door they always go through was locked, so their route was inaccessible. Undaunted, Raven found their way around that obstacle by using a route she had never taken before. Not only that, they made it to biology class on time! Jacob is very proud of Raven—actually he is proud of both of them for the team they are creating and for of all they accomplish in a day. Raven clearly loves her job guiding Jacob, so maybe she is proud of them also. They have built a happy and successful partnership.

How has Jacob so successfully trained Raven to find specific locations? They begin at the door to the destination. Jacob rubs a little cheese or other treat on the door and says, for example, *"Here's biology, here's biology"* (biology is Jacob's favorite subject and his major), and Raven eagerly sniffs the door. She likes the way it smells! Then they back up about six feet, and he says "find *biology*." Raven, leading Jacob, goes to the biology door, and gets a small piece of the treat as a reward. Then they back up several more feet, and go through the process again—find biology, success, treat. Then they back around a corner, then across a street. Every time she finds the door, she gets the treat and they go back a little bit further. They keep going like that until they get back to where they'll regularly be starting from. Then Raven knows exactly what to do when Jacob says, "Find biology." She guides him there without hesitation, tail wagging all the while.

Raven is eager to please, so she memorizes class locations really fast, and she rarely gets off track. Even so, Jacob pays close attention to their surroundings—he needs to know where they are so he'll recognize if they ever do take a wrong turn. He pays attention to the feel of the sidewalk; he notices if there's a curve or a curb where there shouldn't be; he may notice a different smell. If they do end up in the wrong place, he'll say, "Fix it," and Raven will backtrack to the beginning in order to start again. And if they were ever to get truly confused, Jacob could say "Find Mom." Jacob's mom works at the university, and Jacob and Raven ride with her. She always parks in the same place, and Raven knows exactly how to find their way back to Mom's car.

Raven is a bit leery of doors because several times she was hit by one closing and she does not like doors that open on their own, with the use of an automatic door button. She likes Jacob to be in charge of opening the door, so she takes him directly to the door and not to the automatic button. However, there are a couple of doors where she consistently takes Jacob to the automatic button instead of the door itself. Why does she prefer one way over the other for those two doors? Jacob does not know. It is just a decision she has made, for reasons of her own.

With every new semester, Raven and Jacob will have to learn new routes to new classrooms, and next year Jacob will have his own apartment near campus, so that will be a big learning adventure for both of them. Given what he and Raven have accomplished so far, he is confident they will handle that new adventure just fine.

Jacob and Raven's only real problems are caused by people. While most people know that you are supposed to leave an assistance dog alone, and even though Raven's harness has a sign declaring, "Do Not Pet Me. I Am Working," there are people who interfere with them.

It is not unusual for someone to plead, reaching a hand out to Raven, "Oh, I know I'm not supposed to pet your dog, but she's so cute! Can't I just say hi to her?" Those encounters can be confusing for the dog, frustrating for the handler, and even dangerous. One person actually tried to pet Raven while they were crossing the street, which caused Raven to stop in the middle of the road, creating a dangerous situation. Raven is a working dog, and she takes her work very seriously. When people interfere with her, they distract her from her job.

While it is vitally important that people not interfere with an assistance dog, it is equally important that people never allow their dogs to approach an assistance dog. Jacob knows of a guide dog that was attacked by a dog while it was working—attacked by a dog whose owner did not restrain it or control it. That was frightening for both the handler and his guide dog. After that, the guide dog was fearful of other dogs and so could no longer do its job had to be retired. Imagine the upheaval in that handler's life— having their guide dog attacked, having their guide dog lose the ability to work, and having to go through the process of getting a new guide dog. It was an incident that had enormous costs both financially and emotionally. Please, if you have a dog, always have your dog leashed in public. You never know when you will round a corner only to meet someone with an assistance dog.

Remember, if the dog is in a guide dog harness or wearing a cape (service dog vest), you must not touch the dog, talk to the dog, or even look at the dog.

If someone is respectful and does not interfere, but asks Jacob if they can interact with Raven, he will sometimes agree. First, he makes sure that they are in a safe place. Then he removes Raven's harness, which signals to her that she's no longer working. Only then can the person talk to her and pet her. He never allows people to pet her when she is wearing her working harness—being petted by strangers is not part of her job.

Jacob decided he wanted a guide dog when he was sixteen, but Leader Dogs for the Blind,[1] in Michigan, where he got Raven, has a regulation that you must be eighteen to apply. Leader Dogs for the Blind, a nonprofit organization, was founded in 1938 by the Lions Clubs International, which is still involved financially and on the board of Trustees. Leader Dogs breeds and trains the dog, and trains the handler and dog together. Then they offer excellent support when the team is out on its own, and all of this is provided at no cost to the handler. Jacob is extremely grateful for their assistance.

Before Raven, Jacob used a white cane. He said there are many differences between the white cane and Raven, the first thing being curbs. Jacob did not like navigating curbs with his white cane, but with Raven, they are simple. She is faultless with curbs—always letting him know when they are approaching one and carefully guiding him over it.

Jacob also finds that people are more interested in talking to him now. People were shy of him when he had his white cane, but the presence of Raven seems to draw people to him. He is happy to report that he has far more conversations now with others than he did before Raven.

Did I mention the joy that Jacob gets from having Raven in his life? It is clear they love each other, and since Jacob is unable to make eye contact with Raven due to his vision loss, he always has a hand on her. Being a team with Raven has given him confidence in himself—in his ability to get around, in his ability to interact with people, and in his ability to accomplish what he wants in life.

Jacob tells anyone considering getting an assistance dog to make sure they have the time and the willingness to take good care of them. Jacob brushes Raven's teeth, brushes her coat, feeds her, plays with her, and takes her outside for bathroom breaks. Caring for her is a big commitment in time and energy. There is also a financial commitment, including pet insurance and veterinarian visits. Unhesitatingly, Jacob says, "If you've got the time and willingness, a service dog can bring a vast improvement to your life."

References

1. Leader Dogs for the Blind
   https://www.leaderdog.org.

Chapter 3

DOUG, ELLEN, and ILY

*"Having a service dog is a big commitment,
but the rewards are enormous."*

Ily is an all black, half yellow Labrador retriever, half Newfoundland Hearing Assist Dog. She was given her name by a young child who won the privilege to name her in a Can Do Canine's contest. Dogs bred by Can Do Canines are given a letter for each litter of puppies. The puppies in the litter must all have names that begin with the designated letter. Ily was from an "I" litter, and her name stands for "I Love You." Ellen and Doug have had her for just over a year and they do love her. Yes, she is a Hearing Assist Dog for both of them! One dog, two handlers. It is an unusual situation, but not unheard of. It was the same with their first Hearing Assist Dog, Nala. She was with them and helped both of them for thirteen years.

Ily

They first heard about Hearing Assist Dogs at a meeting of the Self Help for Hard of Hearing (SHHH) group. SHHH is now known as Hearing Loss Association of America.[1] A man with his hearing assistance dog came to the meeting and talked about the ways his dog helped him every day. At that time their daughters, who are now grown women, were three and seven years old. Ellen and Doug did not want the girls to have to take on the role of interpreting the world for them, for example telling them every time the phone was ringing. A Hearing Assist Dog seemed like it would be a good idea—and it was.

Ellen and Doug are both people with profound deafness, but they also both have cochlear implants, so they each can hear some things when they are wearing them. A cochlear implant is a high-tech form of hearing aid (although it works on a totally different principle than traditional hearing aids) that can help people recover some of their hearing. One part of the cochlear implant is surgically implanted under the skin above and behind the ear, and a removable part of it sits behind the ear. Like regular hearing aids, the removable part of the cochlear implant is not worn all the time—not in the shower, not in the rain, and not to bed; therefore, Ily's first job of the day is to wake Doug up in the morning when she hears the alarm clock.

Ily alerts Ellen and Doug to all kinds of sounds—doorbell, phone, oven timer, smoke alarm, carbon monoxide alarm, people talking, cars honking, and more. Although the smoke alarm and carbon monoxide alarm seldom or never go off, Ellen and Doug stage drills. Every now and then they activate the alarm, and they reward Ily for alerting them. Ellen jokes that the smoke alarm actually does get used fairly frequently—when she cooks!

Ily needed extra training in order to be a Hearing Assist Dog for both Ellen and Doug, so a trainer from Can Do Canines visited them several times at their home for training sessions. Ily first bonded strongly with Ellen; Doug wondered how well she would be able to bond with him.

Ellen had been feeding Ily, but once Doug took over that duty, it did not take long for Doug and Ily to become solidly bonded too. When Ily first came to live with them, it was hard on Dana, their daughter, who was living with them while she studied to be a veterinary technician. When Ily was being trained, Dana was instructed not to interact with her. She could not even look at her! She had to completely ignore Ily for the entire summer. It was not easy, but she complied. Once Dana was given permission to interact with Ily, they became solid friends. Now they are family.

Assistance dogs are sometimes called on to do something they have not been specifically trained to do. Doug loves to canoe. In fact, he likes to make solo trips into the Boundary Waters Canoe Area Wilderness in Northern Minnesota. Ily will soon begin learning how to be a good canoeing and camping partner! That may be something of a challenge for her, since she does not like to swim, even though both Labradors and Newfoundlands are known as dogs who love to be in the water. Hopefully, she will be a good enough canoeing partner that they will not end up in the water! She is not afraid of water, and she will swim if she is coaxed enough, but she is not really thrilled about it. Ellen speculates that is because she spent so much time in prison as a puppy.

Yes, prison! Can Do Canines has arrangements with seven prisons in Minnesota and Wisconsin for inmates to socialize the young dogs. Each of the facilities takes between five and twenty puppies at one time. Selected inmates are assigned to each dog, and a Can Do Canines trainer makes regular visits to instruct the inmate handlers how to work with the dogs. The puppies receive good socialization and they are also taught some basic commands. The COVID pandemic restrictions caused the program to be suspended for a time. The inmates and the Can Do Canines trainers, not to mention the dogs, were delighted when it was able to start up again.

Ellen and Doug's first Hearing Assist Dog, Nala, a yellow Labrador retriever, found skills outside of what she had been trained to do. Ellen started to notice that Nala was always right next to her. No matter where she was or what she was doing, Nala was always right there, in light contact with her. This went on for quite a while and Ellen started to worry. Maybe something was wrong with Nala and she was trying to tell Ellen. To be safe, she took Nala to the veterinary clinic. They checked her over thoroughly, but they could find nothing amiss. Nevertheless, Nala persisted with this unusual behavior. Then Ellen discovered that she had breast cancer. It was not that something had been wrong with Nala; it was that something had been wrong with Ellen! Nala knew it and had tried to tell Ellen. Nala continued to stay close until one day, when Ellen was just about done with chemotherapy, Nala completely stopped that behavior. At her next doctor's visit, Ellen learned that the cancer was in remission. She already knew that because when Nala had gone back to being her old self, Ellen knew that the cancer scare was over.

Having a Hearing Assist Dog has made both Doug and Ellen's lives much better. Doug feels having Ily with him makes his disability visible. Before, when out shopping for instance, people would be talking to him but he could not hear them and they would become irritated. With Ily by his side, it is clear to everyone that he is not being difficult, but is someone with a disability. Having a

Hearing Assist Dog has allowed them both to be more open about their disability—they do not feel ashamed or "less than" others. Being out with a Hearing Assist Dog is a good way to educate people about disabilities in general and hearing impairment specifically.

Ellen said that being hearing impaired used to be more of a stigma, although there seems to be more acceptance now of people's differences. People with hearing loss used to be characterized as "stupid" or "slow-witted." Ellen did not like to be out in the world when people had those attitudes but she says now she is glad to be in the world, and she is glad to be able to educate people about hearing impairment and about assistance dogs. She gives thanks to Ily—she is proud of Ily and she is proud of herself. She says thirty years ago, she never would have dreamed that she could have such a rich and fulfilling life.

Another benefit of having Ily is walking; they have to be sure that Ily is healthy and fit. They feed her well, brush her teeth, brush her coat, and get plenty of exercise. Ily loves to play fetch, which gives her important play time. Ellen also typically walks five miles a day with Ily. With Ily at her side, Ellen says she is not nervous about walking at night.

Nala, their first assistance dog, died after thirteen years with Ellen and Doug. Ellen said, "I knew I was going to be sad, but I was shocked at how heart-broken I was. It took four years before I was ready to get another service dog." But it turned out that the timing was just right, because when Ellen was ready, so was Ily.

References

1. "Our Founder," Hearing Loss Association of America, accessed May 6, 2022, https://www.hearingloss.org/about-hlaa/our-founder/.

Chapter 4

BRETT and BARBIE

"Every diabetic should have a service dog!"

One slow day at work, Brett and a coworker were looking at the news online when they came upon a story about a diabetes assistance dog. Brett has had diabetes his entire life, but he had never heard of such assistance dogs and was intrigued. He spent a few days on the internet (not at work!) learning everything he could about diabetes assistance dogs. The first thing he learned was that trained assistance dogs cost a lot of money, an unrealistic amount of money for most people, but especially for people who are disabled and on a fixed income. Unfortunately, medical insurance will not help with any expenses related to assistance dogs. That was disappointing news, but Brett kept looking and happily he came across information on Can Do Canines, a nonprofit assistance dog organization in Minnesota. Can Do Canines does not charge people for assistance dogs. Brett decided to apply for a Diabetes Assist Dog.

The Can Do Canines vetting process was extensive. Representatives visited Brett at his home three times. They videotaped an interview with him, they videotaped the house and the yard, and they requested Brett's medical records. They told him if he were to be approved for a Diabetes Assist Dog, it could take as long as a year before there was a dog for him. But luck was with him, because in four months, he got the call that he was approved. Not only that, they had a Diabetes Assist Dog ready for him!

The dog that would be Brett's had just completed three years of training to be an agency-certified Diabetes Assist Dog. But Brett had to be certified, too. He went to the Can Do Canines facility, where he stayed in their visitor apartment and spent a week training how to be a Diabetes Assist Dog handler. The first two days were filled with administrative paperwork and training for him without the dog. He was eager to meet the dog, but that wasn't scheduled to happen until day three. Ask as he may, they would not tell him anything about the dog, not even if it was male or female. "We'll get to that," is all they said. Finally, the time came to meet his Diabetes Assist Dog.

First, they told him about her—she was a three-year-old chocolate Labrador retriever and her name was Barbie. He said, "Barbie?" It certainly wasn't a name he would have chosen. "Oh well," he joked, "at least my name isn't Ken!"

Then he met her and for the rest of the week the two of them worked together with a trainer. He was impressed with how much she knew, and how responsive she was to him. On the fourth day, he got to take her back to the apartment. That night, there was a strong thunderstorm, but Barbie remained calm. While Brett was watching TV, Barbie climbed onto the couch, curled up beside him, and fell asleep. He found it soothing and felt happy to have her sleeping next to him. He knew then that Barbie was the right dog for him. At the end of the week, Brett was certified, and they were a team.

According to Can Do Canines protocol, Barbie was tethered to Brett for the first five days they were home. Wherever Brett went, Barbie was with him — at work, even in the bathroom. Only at bedtime was the leash removed. Doing that, Barbie learned that she was to stay with Brett at all times, and Brett learned what it would be like to always have Barbie at his side. The experience created a strong bond between them. No longer just Brett, he had become Brett and Barbie, part of a bonded pair. They have been together now for three years and their bond only grows.

Brett has type-one diabetes. He also has hypoglycemic unawareness, so he does not recognize when his blood sugar is too low, which could result in him losing consciousness. He wears medical devices to keep track of his blood sugar, but Barbie is more sensitive than any of those devices. She smells when his blood sugar is around seventy (getting low) and alerts him, then she watches him to be sure he attends to it. Brett, on the other hand, has to keep up Barbie's training. He keeps a tissue with his scent from a hypoglycemic episode on it in the freezer. For training, he will pretend to have a low blood sugar episode and place the tissue on his body. Barbie makes the connection and gets treats!

Barbie sleeps on the bed next to Brett. One night, not long after Brett first brought her home, she woke him in the middle of the night. His first thought was, "Oh my goodness, this dog has to go out in the middle of the night!" He took her out, wondering if having an assistance dog was going to be such a good idea after all, but Barbie had no interest in anything outside. She was focused solely on Brett, licking and bumping and pawing him. She persisted with this behavior until it finally clicked for Brett—she was telling him his blood sugar was low! They went back in the house and he checked it right away. It was thirty-four—dangerously low. Brett and Barbie had both been sound asleep, but even so, she somehow sensed his low blood sugar, woke him, and kept after him until he understood and tended to it. Brett says, "She sleeps with one nostril open!" Without Barbie's intervention he would have been in very serious medical trouble.

Although Barbie's primary job is to alert Brett when his blood sugar is low, her presence in his life has had many other positive effects. She has gotten him on a good schedule—she wakes him up early for her breakfast and she is insistent that he get up (she loves her breakfast!), which means he is up and going when he might otherwise stay in bed longer than is good for him. Because of Barbie, Brett is healthier—they walk a lot, they play games in the backyard, and they work on upgrading the house. They are busy!

Brett also loves to work in the garden, and Barbie loves being out in the yard with him. In fact, some time ago, she caught a rabbit in the garden. Now, every time they go out to the yard, she runs to that spot and stares, waiting for another rabbit to appear. Ah, but the rabbits are savvy; they have moved on.

Brett enjoys Barbie's company, but it's more than that. He feels a great respect and admiration for her. She has a job to do, an important job, a life and death job, and she does it well.

Brett is proud to be out in public with Barbie, and he is glad to talk to people about her. Most people do not know that assistance dogs help people who have diabetes and they are interested to learn. He enjoys meeting and interacting with new people—interactions he did not have before Barbie.

Living with lifelong diabetes or other chronic diseases is not easy. There can be a sense of grief—a feeling of loss. One can easily become isolated and depressed. Having an assistance dog can give a person back some of the freedom the disease has taken. Assistance dogs help a person to relax and they bring comfort when a person is feeling challenged by the disease. Being with Barbie has certainly lifted Brett's spirits. He is more committed than ever to staying healthy and fit, so he will be around for Barbie for a long time.

Before Barbie came into his life, Brett had been hospitalized many times with low blood sugar. By alerting him to low blood sugar, she has prevented those hospitalizations. He wishes insurance companies realized how much money would be saved if more people had assistance dogs, how many ambulance trips and hospital stays would be avoided. Assistance dogs truly are a form of preventive medicine. As Brett says, "Every diabetic should have a service dog!"

Chapter 5

Kevin and Scrappy Boo

"Scrappy Boo opened up the world for me."

Kevin did not intend to get an assistance dog, he just wanted a pal, and when he first saw Scrappy Boo, who was six weeks old, he knew that this was the dog who would be his pal. They had an immediate bond. Scrappy Boo is thirteen now, and he and Kevin have been together the entire time.

Kevin says there was life before Scrappy Boo, and there is life with Scrappy Boo—that's how much he has changed things for Kevin. In fact, it was Kevin's doctor, seeing what a difference Scrappy Boo made in his life, who suggested that he should be recognized as a psychiatric service dog.*

Kevin suffers from post-traumatic stress disorder, as well as emphysema and kidney disease. He has had multiple hospitalizations for depression. There were days when he could not convince himself to get out of bed. He says, "It was very, very, very difficult for me to ever leave the house," but then Scrappy Boo arrived. Now Kevin leaves the house every day! Not only do they get up and go outside together every morning for Scrappy Boo's morning bathroom break, they are out and about a lot. They are a recognizable duo at the grocery store, at the library, at the doctor's office—all around town. Their special bond is evident to even a casual observer, with Scrappy Boo's attention always focused on Kevin.

Kevin trained Scrappy Boo to do many things, and it was easy, because Scrappy Boo had naturally stepped into his role of psychiatric assistance dog. It was as though he'd been born to do it. He licks Kevin's face when he is extremely depressed or is about to have an anxiety attack, and he persists licking until Kevin makes a move to remedy the situation—to get his medication or to interact with Scrappy Boo. The main training Kevin had to do was to reward Scrappy Boo for what he instinctively knew how to do. Yes, Kevin trained Scrappy Boo, but Scrappy Boo also trained Kevin—he trained Kevin to depend on him, trained Kevin to trust him, and trained Kevin to allow himself to be guided by him when Kevin is depressed or anxious.

Kevin says that while medication certainly helps him, having Scrappy Boo really has made all the difference in his life. No more hospitalizations! No more days spent in bed! He reports he has tried many other interventions, but nothing has worked like Scrappy Boo. When you see them together, it is clear that Scrappy Boo keeps a very close eye on Kevin. He cheers him up when he needs cheering and he calms him down when he needs calming.

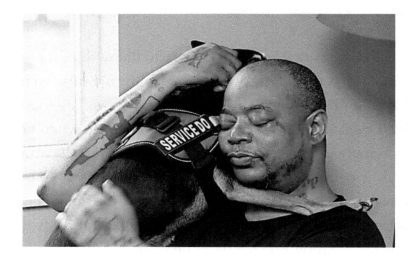

Kevin is aware that Scrappy Boo is getting older, and when the time comes that he cannot do his job easily, Kevin hopes to go through an agency to find a young assistance dog. Although Kevin trained Scrappy Boo to meet Americans with Disabilities Act[1] service dog requirements, he does not think he has the energy to train another assistance dog by himself. He hopes he will be able to find a dog as loving and intelligent and good natured as Scrappy Boo. Scrappy Boo may soon retire his psychiatric assistance dog duties, but he will never retire the bond he shares with Kevin.

Kevin encourages people to look into having an assistance dog. "Check into it," he says, "your quality of life can be greatly improved."

Note: Scrappy Boo passed away August 2, 2021
at the age of fourteen and a half.

*From the Americans with Disabilities Act (ADA): **"Service animals are defined as dogs that are individually trained to do work or perform tasks for people with disabilities.** Examples of such work or tasks include guiding people who are blind, alerting people who are deaf, pulling a wheelchair, alerting and protecting a person who is having a seizure, reminding a person with mental illness to take prescribed medications, calming a person with Post Traumatic Stress Disorder (PTSD) during an anxiety attack, or performing other duties. Service animals are working animals, not pets. The work or task a dog has been trained to provide must be directly related to the person's disability. Dogs whose sole function is to provide comfort or emotional support do not qualify as service animals under the ADA".

References

1. "ADA requirements: Service Animals: How "Service Animal" is Defined." The Department of Justice, accessed May 6, 2022, https:www.ada.gov/service_animals_2010.htm

Chapter 6

JEAN and LEXIE

"It's been a wonderful experience to have Lexie."

Jean got Lexie, her first Hearing Assist Dog, in the autumn of 2007, when Lexie was just a few days shy of her first birthday. Lexie is fourteen now.

Lexie came through Hearing and Service Dogs of Minnesota, which is now called Can Do Canines. This was before Can Do Canines had its own breeding program, and many dogs were donated to the organization. Lexie was one of them.

Jean, who lost her hearing when she was three years old, was living in Texas with her mother when she first learned of Hearing Assist Dogs. She found an organization in Austin that trained them, but the cost of getting one, even though subsidized, was just too much. Jean never let go of the idea of one day having a Hearing Assist Dog, and when she moved to Minnesota after her mother died, she kept looking. She found Hearing and Service Dogs of Minnesota, applied for a Hearing Assist Dog, was accepted, and was soon partnered with Lexie. They graduated from training in May of 2008. Jean is proud of the fact that she was in the same graduating class with Can Do Canine's first Autism Assist Dog team.

At that time, all training by Can Do Canines was done at the handler's residence. A field trainer visited Jean's home once a week. Lexie was trained to alert Jean when she heard the doorbell, a knock on the door, the telephone, fire alarm, alarm clock, or an intruder outside. In between these official training sessions, neighbors would help by knocking on the door or even peering in the window, pretending to be an intruder. When Lexie heard any of those things, she would go to Jean and touch her, then lead her to where the sound was coming from. Cheers and treats followed. They also worked in public places with the trainer, so that Lexie could learn not be distracted by people and noise, and Jean could learn to rely on Lexie. In addition, they went to obedience training at Pet Smart, which at the time offered free training for assistance dogs and their handlers.

Jean's life totally changed when Lexie came to her. Even though she had graduated from college in 2005, with a bachelor of science in human development and family studies and a minor in American Sign Language, she felt isolated and was afraid to go out much. She said when you have hearing loss, communicating is challenging, and it is challenging to know how to fit in with others and how to make friends. Lexie changed all that: "Lexie taught me social skills!"

Now, instead of just going to work and then going home, Jean is very busy with volunteer work. She is an active member of the Lion's Club, and she does a lot of public speaking on behalf of Can Do Canines. In fact, she occupies a leadership position with the Lion's Club. Around town, she is known as "The Dog Lady." She's been recognized several times in restaurants or stores by people who had been in the audience for one of her speaking events.

Besides public speaking for Can Do Canines, Jean excels at fundraising for them by selling chocolates. One year, she received Can Do Canine's "Top Dog" award for being the fundraiser who raised the most money that year. Can Do Canines is important to Jean not just as an avenue for volunteer activities, but the staff, volunteers, and graduates of the organization are an extended family for her. Jean is full of admiration for the work of Can Do Canines and is aware of the great benefit people receive from the organization. She feels good to be able to help Can Do Canines in any way possible, and you will find her volunteering at most of their events.

In 2012, Jean got her first cochlear implant, enabling her to hear most sounds. That made a huge difference in her life. In 2015, she received her second one for the other ear. While Jean can now hear, her hearing is not perfect, and she does not wear her cochlear implants all the time. Lexie still provides important assistance. For instance, there was the time that the carbon monoxide alarm went off at eleven o'clock at night. Jean was in bed, without her cochlear implants on, so she did not hear it. Lexie alerted her and led her to the source of the sound. It turned out that the alarm just needed new batteries, but it could have been much worse.

Jean works at a large store. She only works four-hour shifts, and since Lexie is getting old, Jean does not take Lexie to work with her. Jean's coworkers are aware that she has a hearing impairment, so they keep an eye on her; however, that is not a foolproof arrangement. One time, when there was a tornado in the vicinity, a public address announcement told everyone to go to the back of the store. As usual, Jean heard the sound of the announcement but did not understand the individual words. She kept working, until she noticed that there were no customers in the aisles, so she went to the back stock room to find out what was going on. In the excitement her coworkers had forgotten to alert her!

Jean does take Lexie with her when she shops, and this brings up the controversial subject of "fake service dogs." Jean was shopping with Lexie, who, as always, was wearing her Can Do Canines assistance dog cape or vest. A shopper had a small dog, wearing a service dog vest (the type from the internet), in her cart. When the dog saw Lexie, it started to bark and yip wildly. The dog's owner could not silence it. Assistance dogs are trained to perform specific tasks for a person with disability but they also must behave in public and be under their handler's control. One reason Jean is such an active advocate for Can Do Canines is to let people know exactly what an assistance dog really is. Another reason she wants to get the word out about assistance dogs is so the many people who would benefit from having one can learn about them and hopefully get the assistance they need and deserve.

Jean signing "I love you" to Lexie

As Lexie ages, Jean is careful not to overwork her. Jean takes exceptionally good care of Lexie, who eats a prescription dog food for a medical condition and which is quite expensive—but Jean says Lexie must have the best! Visits to the veterinarian are a regular part of their routine, but not every visit has to do with a medical treatment. When Lexie first went to the veterinary clinic, she was nervous so the veterinarian suggested that they come in for "happy visits." So for a while, Jean brought Lexie to the clinic once a week where the staff would greet her happily with much petting and exclaiming. Then they would walk her around the clinic, weigh her, and give her a treat. Lexie then loved the veterinary clinic! She also loves her Doggy Daycare, which she sometimes visits when Jean is at work, and where there is also much petting and exclaiming, as well as play time with other dogs. It is a good life

Jean tells all this to people when she is speaking about assistance dogs. She wants people to know about assistance dogs so they can have one if they need one, but she also wants them to know that having an assistance dog is a big responsibility. You must be sure you can physically and financially take care of the dog, clean up after the dog, learn the dog's limits to avoid overworking it, and make sure it is always safe. The cost of training an assistance dog can be up to forty-five thousand dollars, so you do not want to do anything that could harm the dog's ability to do their job. Jean says, "Having a service dog is a big commitment in time and money, but it's worth every minute and every penny."

Fortunately The International Association of Assistance Dog Partners (IAADP) offers some help with the financial commitment of having an assistance dog. They award grants for dog care such as allergy medicine and monthly flea and tick medicine. In order to be a member of IAADP, a person must attest that their assistance dog meets or exceeds IAADP's Minimum Training Standards.[1] Those standards are listed in the introduction to this book.

Jean knows what she will do after Lexie dies—she will apply for a successor Hearing Assist Dog. The benefits, in terms of safety, and just being able to live a full life, are so great that Jean cannot imagine life without an assistance dog.

Note: Sadly Lexie passed away on October 10, 2020, at the age of fourteen. Jean is not quite ready for a successor Hearing Assist Dog, but since she loves dogs, she is fostering Can Do Canine dogs who are finishing their training and need "real world" experience. Currently, Jean is working with Yasmin, a young, yellow Labrador retriever. The foster dogs usually stay with Jean anywhere from a few days to a few weeks and go everywhere with Jean, who has fun planning their outings. It is another way Jean gives back to an organization that has given her, and many others, so much.

Jean and Yasmin (photo courtesy of Jean with permission from Can Do Canines for Yasmin)

References

1. "Minimum Training Standards for Public Access," International Association of Assistance Dog Partners, accessed May 5, 2022, https://www.iaadp.org/iaadp-minimum-training-standards-for-public-access.html.

Chapter 7

JOHN and MAJOR

"He is a very good guy! He's smart, he's dedicated, and he's highly competent."

One of the first things you notice when you see John, who has a vision impairment, and Major, a yellow Labrador retriever, is that Major is fast! Which is exactly what John wants. When it was time for Cody, his previous guide dog, to retire, John contacted The Seeing Eye[1], in Morristown, New Jersey. John says it is the best school in the world! Major is his seventh guide dog and all of his dogs except his first one came from The Seeing Eye. He told them that he wanted a "highly energetic, driven dog." John himself is fast, so he prefers a dog that is energetic and fast, one that he can gradually train to slow down if he needs to do so. It's easier to train a fast dog to be slower than it is to train a slow dog to be faster. At first, John had to put booties on Major because he was so driven, and he pushed off so hard that he was tearing up the pads on his feet, especially his back feet. He is learning to slow down a bit, and his feet are fine, although he is still quite quick. Just what John likes.

John said it can take a good year to build an excellent working relationship. There was a period of focused training for them, because Major was very "dog-distracted" at first. One time, early on, he saw another dog and headed toward it, pulling John off balance. John tripped and fell. Major learned something from that, and since then he has been much better about ignoring other dogs. John does have to correct him sometimes, by giving a quick flick on the leash. It is not a punishment; it doesn't in any way hurt

Major, it is simply a way to get his attention back to the work at hand.

When John first got Major, they were going to the office five days a week. Major loved commuting on the light rail, he enjoyed being at the office, and he was happy on the trip home. Then COVID pandemic restrictions were put in place and John started mostly working from home, with only occasional trips to the office. Being the energetic, driven dog he is, Major was not pleased with the inaction, and he put on a few pounds. John remedied that in two ways. First, accompanied by a friend, he takes Major to a dog park several times per week. There, Major goes from being an energetic working dog to being an energetic playing dog. Secondly, a few times a week, John will take his Global Positioning System, set a location they have never been to, and off they will go on a new adventure. Major and John are both happier not being cooped up in the apartment, and Major's weight is back down to a perfect fifty-seven pounds.

John and Major do sometimes disagree. They will come to a corner where John thinks they should turn right, but Major insists that they should continue straight. Sometimes Major gives in, but if he is adamant, John gives in. Major is not always right, but nearly always.

John remembers a time with his black Labrador guide dog. They were on a street that John knew well, cruising along, everything fine, when his dog suddenly and forcefully veered out into the street, pulling a surprised John along. Someone was backing out of their driveway, fast and without looking. If not for the dog's quick action, they would have been directly behind the car.

John is planning on a Caribbean cruise in June, and it will not be his first. He enjoys cruises—he likes the food, and being a musician himself, he enjoys the live music. John plays electric bass, and before the COVID pandemic, he played in a band at church and in clubs around town. He hopes to get back to performing soon. When on the cruise, he gets a room with a balcony so he and Major can enjoy the sea air. Major did need to learn one new thing for his first cruise and that was to use the "potty box," which is usually located in a maintenance room, out of the way of passengers. Major learned that quicker than any of John's previous dogs. Major is quick in more ways than just one!

John provided a picture of him and his previous dog
Cody enjoying one of their cruises.

There was one unpleasant experience on a cruise
when a woman, saying, "I know I'm not supposed to do
this, but I just have to," went ahead and reached to pet
Major. John had to grab her hand to stop her, saying, "No,
you may not pet him. He's working." The woman was
highly offended to not have her way. John says it is not

unusual for people to do that—claim that they know they are not supposed to do something but then do it anyway. It gets tiresome, but John says he knows they do not intend harm. Sometimes he will stop to educate them, sometimes he will just move on.

John is also a Ham radio operator. He recently obtained his general class license so he can talk to people all over the world. Soon he will be moving to a new apartment and he has been training Major how to get there from various locations. One day they went up to the new apartment door then turned to leave and Major turned to look at him, as if to say, "You wanted to come here. We're here. And now you want to leave right away?" John laughed, but insisted that they turn around. Then a voice called, "Major?" The person calling out was a Ham radio friend of John's. They had never met in person, but he had heard about Major and wondered if this could possibly be him. He invited John and Major in for coffee, so Major was vindicated—it truly had not been time to just turn around and leave! John's new apartment promises to be just right—a friend as a neighbor, a balcony that will improve his Ham radio reception, and a big plus for John—a coffee room with unlimited coffee.

Major is a young dog, so retirement is years away. But when the time comes, John will find a good home for him, as he has for all his retired guide dogs. And he will remember Major as one of the best.

References

1. The Seeing Eye. Website:
   https://www.seeingeye.org

Chapter 8
MIKE and CHARLIE

"January 2, 2016 is the day my life totally changed.
That's the day I got Charlie."

It was Mike's doctor who suggested he look into getting an assistance dog. Mike has type-one diabetes, along with hypoglycemic unawareness, which means he does not sense when his blood sugar falls too low. Because he does not feel it, he passes out, which results in an ambulance trip to the hospital. It is a serious condition so an assistance dog could literally save his life.

Mike had not known there were Diabetes Assist Dogs and he was excited by the idea of having one. However, when he started researching assistance dogs, he was stunned by the cost. A service dog could cost up to forty-five thousand dollars! Medical insurance does not pay anything. Clearly, it was not an option for him. Still, he persevered with his research and luckily came across Can Do Canines, a nonprofit assistance dog organization in Minnesota that does not charge for assistance dogs. He applied to Can Do Canines, and the fifty dollar application fee was the only fee he ever had to pay them. They told him, "All we want is a thank you." Mike has plenty of those to give as he holds Can Do Canines in the highest esteem.

Charlie now and then

Charlie, a golden retriever, was bred specifically to be an assistance dog by a breeder associated with Can Do Canines. When the dogs are young, they live for a while at local prisons, where inmates socialize them and teach them common commands. When the dogs are two years old, their natural abilities and inclinations are assessed by Can Do Canine trainers to determine what kind of assistance dog they will be—a Diabetes Assist Dog, like Charlie; a Hearing Assist Dog; a Mobility Assist Dog; an Autism Assist Dog; or a Seizure Assist Dog. The dogs then go through about a year of training in order to become accomplished and specialized assistance dogs.

When Mike's application was accepted, he was placed on a waiting list. He had no idea how long he would have to wait, since there was no telling when a dog with the special aptitude and training for smelling low blood sugar would become available. Happily, he was only on the list for a year. He met Charlie for the first time at the Can Do Canine facility, where they trained together for a week, and where their life as a team began.

Charlie accompanies Mike everywhere, and he is known and loved wherever they go. Charlie seems to know that people love him, and it makes him a happy and proud dog. There is a spring to his step and his tail is always wagging. What really makes Charlie happy though are drive-through windows, such as at the pharmacy and the bank, because when that drawer opens, there is always a treat for Charlie. Oh, Charlie does love his treats!

Mike has far more independence since Charlie came to be with him. Before there was Charlie, Mike's coworkers had had to learn to recognize when his blood sugar was low so they could alert him. But what if they did not notice in time? Mike would pass out and end up in the hospital. At home, Mike's wife, Teresa, could keep an eye on him, but she could not be with him every minute. It is a good thing Charlie can be with him—and Charlie is. He is with Mike all the time—in the car, in a store, at work, on a walk, at the doctor's office, in bed—everywhere. Now Teresa is able to leave home without worrying because Charlie is there to watch over Mike and keep him safe. Charlie gives both Mike and Teresa great peace of mind. He is truly a lifesaver. Teresa calls Charlie "Mike's Miracle."

Mike's Miracle

Teresa loves Charlie, too, but she is careful not to let him get too attached to her. Charlie is an assistance dog, and his bond is and must be with Mike and only Mike. For example, Mike is the only one who grooms him, which Charlie enjoys, and the only one who feeds him, which Charlie enjoys even more. Charlie loves to eat! He eats twice a day, and without fail, when it is time to eat, Charlie sits next to his food dish and stares at Mike. Not only can Charlie smell low blood sugar, he can tell time!

When Charlie does smell that Mike's blood sugar is low, he barks at Mike. Charlie never barks, unless he needs to urge Mike to tend to his low blood sugar. That is how he has been trained. During our interview, which took place outside in a busy city park with many distractions and noises, Charlie barked. Mike and I kept talking, not really heeding Charlie. Charlie waited a minute or so, and when he saw that Mike was not taking any action, he barked and kept barking. Mike realized that Charlie was telling him to check his blood sugar, which he did. While it was still in the safe range, it was going down. Sometimes when his blood sugar is dropping, it will self-adjust and be fine. More often, it will keep dropping. Mike says, "Charlie will let me know. He'll take care of it." A bit later, Charlie barked again. Sure enough, Mike's blood sugar had fallen further. It had not fallen to a dangerous level, but without Charlie's intervention it likely would have. Charlie kept an eye on Mike until he took care of it by eating glucose drops, then he relaxed.

At home, there is a tug device attached to the refrigerator door so Charlie can open it, and another tug on one of the crisper drawers, where cans of Mountain Dew are kept. When Charlie lets Mike know that his blood sugar is low, Mike will say, "Get a juice." Charlie goes to the refrigerator, uses the tug to open the door, then pulls open the crisper drawer, grabs a can of Mountain Dew in his mouth, and carries it to Mike. Once he sees Mike open the can, he returns to the refrigerator, closes the crisper drawer, and closes the refrigerator. Mike says, "I'm a very,

very lucky person to have Charlie in my life. He amazes me every day."

Like so many people with assistance dogs, Mike has found that he has to do a lot of educating—not of Charlie, but of people. Many people do not know they are not supposed to interact with an assistance dog and Mike has to teach them. Laughing, he says, "Have you ever tried to tell a five-year-old that she can't pet your dog?" Most people do not intend to be a nuisance, and they are grateful to learn how to properly interact with a person and their assistance dog.

Mike and his wife live in an apartment where dogs are not allowed. But legally, under the Americans with Disabilities Act,[1] service dogs cannot be refused, so Mike had to educate his landlord. There was no problem—once the landlord knew the law, he readily agreed to have the dog.

Mike and Teresa once went to a restaurant for dinner, and of course Charlie was with them, wearing his Can Do Canines assistance dog cape as he always does outside the apartment. The host told them that they could not enter, that dogs were not allowed. Mike explained that Charlie was a Diabetic Assist Dog, explained the law, and showed the worker their paperwork (which is always in a pocket in Charlie's cape and includes his Can Do Canine certification along with emergency contacts), but they were still refused. Fortunately, Mike is easy going, and he knows that a friendly explanation will get him further than an angry one. He asked to see the manager, then explained again. They were seated with no fuss. As in any restaurant, once they were seated, Mike commanded Charlie "under," and Charlie spent the entire time lying under Mike's chair.

One time Mike and Teresa (and Charlie) had to fly somewhere. Not knowing the correct protocol, Mike called the Transportation Security Administration (TSA) ahead of time. Mike says, "They couldn't have been more helpful." They took all the information about the flight and about where they were staying, then TSA agents actually picked them up at their motel. Once at the airport, they were escorted past the long line and through the scanner. Mike smiles, "We did have to take our shoes off, though."

Can Do Canines assistance dogs will typically work between five and seven years. Then they will be retired, and Can Do Canines will find a permanent home for the dog so the person can get another assistance dog. Mike says that one of Can Do Canine stipulations is that you cannot have any other dogs in the house. At the time he applied to Can Do Canines, Mike and Teresa had a Saint Bernard. When Mike's application was approved, they had to find a new home for their Saint Bernard. That was sad, but they knew Mike would be getting a dog that would not only be his full-time companion, but in all likelihood would be his lifesaver, and Charlie has been his lifesaver.

Mike hopes he can keep Charlie once he has been retired, even though he would not be a Diabetes Assist Dog any longer. Of course, if he is not an assistance dog he will not qualify to stay in the apartment. Plus, Mike will have to see if he can get another Diabetes Assist Dog and still keep Charlie. It is a conundrum for sure. But there is time, and it is a problem that Mike fully intends to solve.

References

1. "Americans with Disabilities Act Requirements: Service Animals," U.S. Department of Justice, 2010, https://www.ada.gov/service_animals_2010.htm

Chapter 9

KELLI and JUSTEEN

commonly known as Teenie

"It feels like a miracle that we're together."

Kismet. That is the word Kelli uses to describe the circumstances that conspired to bring her and Teenie together.

Kelli's Parkinson's disease (a progressive neurological disease affecting movement) symptoms were progressing. She had just had her fourth back surgery and her dog, her beloved companion Skye, was at the end of her life. Kelli was crying on the day she left the veterinary clinic, having finally accepted the fact that Skye was nearing the end of her life. At that time, Kelli felt that she only wanted to live long enough to be with Skye when she crossed the "Rainbow Bridge."[1] As fate would have it, as she was leaving the clinic, a woman with a large black dog in a red, black, and white assistance dog cape was entering. The woman had a compassionate heart, and seeing Kelli's distress, offered to talk. It was a life-changing conversation. Kelli went home and applied to Can Do Canines for a Mobility Assist Dog.

Meanwhile, Teenie had been bred and trained by the Guide Dog Foundation[2] but was deemed not assertive enough to be a guide dog for the blind. Can Do Canines had accepted her and begun the process of retraining.

Kelli applied to Can Do Canines on the seventeenth of November. Two days later, on the nineteenth of November, Teenie arrived at Can Do Canines for training. The next May, Skye passed away. Ten days after Skye died, Teenie finished her training, and she and Kelli were introduced. They have been together for six years. Timing is everything!

Kelli says that before Teenie, she felt like she was living in a tornado. Her husband would come home from work and there would be fifteen things on the floor for him to pick up—dimes, stamps, credit cards, forks, and clothing. Now Teenie picks them all up as they fall so Kelli's husband can come home, change his clothes, and go for his run. He is a marathon runner and as he trains, he runs with Teenie—typically three miles every day.

One of the things Teenie frequently has to pick up is Kelli's medicine bottle. Kelli keeps her pills in a bottle, within a bottle, within a bottle, so there is absolutely no chance that Teenie will get at the actual pills. When Teenie hears something drop, she is right there to pick it up. For safety, she has been taught that when she hears or sees the actual pills fall to the floor, she must leave the room.

Teenie was also trained to help Kelli get dressed and undressed. She helps first by getting clothing from drawers and bringing them to Kelli. Then she helps to tug Kelli's clothes on and tug them up. Later, she will tug them off and put them in the laundry hamper. When it's laundry time, she'll carry the hamper to the laundry room, and finally, she removes the clothes from the dryer. Teenie helps with all manner of household chores and activities.

During the time Kelli and Teenie have been together, Kelli has had fourteen surgeries. She cannot imagine how she would have managed without Teenie. Her husband would have had to quit his job and become her full-time caregiver. That simply would not have been feasible. Her partnership with Teenie allowed them each some independence. Teenie's help is indispensable.

Somehow, Teenie has learned to do things she was not trained to do—like tell time. Kelli takes her Parkinson's medication on a regular schedule with the use of a timer, but she does not always hear the timer. One day while working in the garden—Kelli is an avid and excellent gardener—she noticed that Teenie was staring at her. She was standing really close to Kelli and just staring at her. Teenie loves green beans, so Kelli thought she wanted one and offered it to her. Teenie refused to take it. She would stare at Kelli, then walk to the back door. When Kelli didn't follow, she would return, stare at her, then again walk to the back door. Over and over she did this, until finally Kelli got up and followed her into the house. There was Kelli's medicine bottle on the kitchen counter and she realized she was late taking it. As hard as it was to fathom, Teenie had been urging her into the house so she could take her medication!

Teenie also taught herself to recognize when Kelli's blood pressure is going to be low. Not when it *has* dropped, but when it is *going* to drop. It took Kelli some time to realize that when Teenie would put her paw on Kelli's lap and stare at her, she was telling her to be extra careful when she stood up. The first few times Teenie did this with her paw, Kelli just did not understand, and when she stood, her blood pressure plummeted and she fell. Teenie was telling her that there was trouble on the horizon so to be careful while standing up. Kelli has learned to pay very close attention to Teenie's signals.

One wonders how Teenie taught herself to predict falling blood pressure or maybe the ensuing falls—changes in body chemistry smells, keen observation, or something else? However she did it, to Kelli it seems like a miracle. She says of Teenie, "She is much more aware of what's happening to me than I ever was or ever will be."

Teenie goes shopping with Kelli. There was a time when the grocery store was unusually busy. Waiting in line at the register, Kelli got her little wallet with all her credit cards out of her purse so she'd be ready when she got to the register. Then she dropped it and credit cards scattered everywhere! One by one, Teenie went about picking credit cards up from the floor. She managed to get ten, but the eleventh one gave her trouble. Good dog that she is, she persisted until she finally got it. Kelli was so proud of her!

Teenie also helps Kelli by providing "momentum pulls." Kelli will sometimes get stalled when walking and Teenie will gently move forward, giving Kelli the momentum to get going again. As the Parkinson's disease increasingly stalls Kelli's motion, these momentum pulls become more and more important.

Workers in the stores where they regularly shop know Teenie. Because of Parkinson's, Kelli drags one foot and she does sometimes fall. The workers know that if Teenie comes up to them alone, they must follow her, because Kelli has fallen and needs help

The main problem they encounter in stores is what Kelli calls "drive-by petting." Teenie walks on Kelli's left side, because she uses a cane with her right hand. While "keep to the right" is the norm when shopping with a grocery cart, Kelli has taken to keeping to the left of the aisle, in order to keep Teenie between the cart and the shelves. That way Teenie is protected from people who would attempt to pet her. Teenie always wears her service dog cape when they are out, but it does not deter everyone from reaching for her. Kelli says that there are days when she has the physical and mental ability to stop and educate people, but there are also days when she cannot have those interactions, so she must get what she needs and get out of the store quickly.

Children are naturally drawn to Teenie. If a child asks its mother before approaching, and if the mother responds by asking Kelli, she will, when she feels able to, allow the child to pet Teenie. She explains to the child that a dog in a cape is a superhero on a special job and they must never be touched without permission. Kelli carries suckers in her purse, and if all goes well with the child and parent, she will give the child a sucker and thank them for being respectful.

It saddens Kelli though that some people who are attracted to Teenie do not seem to want to interact with Kelli, only with Teenie. Could it be that they are afraid to interact with a person with disabilities? Kelli says "Look me in the eye, acknowledge me. I am you, just living a different story... I am more than my disability, I have abilities, many of them, but I need you to see me first to know they exist." So if you happen to see Kelli and Teenie, smile and say "hello." You'll meet a fascinating person and maybe find some common ground!

Kelli and Teenie both enjoy being in nature, and in the summertime, they can often be found strolling through the Minnesota Arboretum or a local park. Being out in nature renews Kelli, cheers and calms her. Some days though Kelli is confined to the house due to her pain. Then, with Teenie at her side, she might write poetry. Or

she will keep in touch with other Can Do Canine graduates on their Facebook page where graduates share anec-
dotes, give and receive advice, and generally support one
another. The support of others is an important tool for
navigating life as a person with disabilities—a person
with an assistance dog. Kelli says, "I cannot express how
grateful I am to have Teenie in my life. More than grateful.
There aren't words to express my thankfulness. Now I
have freedom and safety that I didn't have before."

Here is an excerpt from Kelli's poem "Spun" (2019, unpublished), printed with her permission:

Am I spun glass
a bounty of prisms
clarity expressed in vivid reflections of my heart's purity
strength despite fragility
a precarious state of being…
could this be my heart's desire
demonstrating to the world
my worth
my strength
beautiful shards cracking me open" …

References

1. "…the idea of the rainbow bridge may have roots that date back to ancient times, pet lovers have essentially rediscovered it in the past few decades thanks to a poem that describes a bridge pets cross over to a happy afterlife when they die."

   a. Joe Oliveto, "30 Popular Rainbow Bridge Poems for Deceased Pets," Cake, September 21, 2021, https://www.joincake.com/blog/rainbow-bridge-poems/

2. Guide Dog Foundation, https://www.guidedog.org

Chapter 10
LEN and ROGUE

"The nose knows!"

Len lived with diabetes for fifty-seven years and he was confident that he had gotten pretty good at managing it—until he regained consciousness in his living room, surrounded by emergency medical personnel. His partner had returned home to find him unconscious in his recliner. That was not the first time she had to call 9-1-1.

Len knew he had to do something, so he went to see his doctor. Perhaps it was time to have an internal automatic insulin pump installed. One thing the doctor suggested was a conversation with the diabetes educator, who asked him if he had ever considered getting an assistance dog. Len said, "A service dog? Why would I need a service dog? I get around just fine. My eyesight is good, my hearing is good. No, I've never considered getting a service dog." She told him she was referring to a Diabetes Assist Dog. He had no idea, had never heard of such a thing. So she told him what the dogs do and she suggested he look into Can Do Canines.

He suspected that having a Diabetes Assist Dog would force him out into the open as someone with diabetes and he was not sure how he would deal with that. He had lived with diabetes all his life, but no one outside of his family knew about it. It just was not talked about thirty or forty years ago. Before the Americans with Disabilities Act became law in 1990, having a disability was considered by many to be tantamount to having a character flaw. If a person had a disability that they could hide, they did hide it. Plus, Len is naturally a very private person; nonetheless, he took a deep breath and bent to the task of learning what he could about Diabetes Assist Dogs and about Can Do Canines.

His research results about Can Do Canines were nothing but positive, even glowing, so he went for a visit and was favorably impressed. Then he attended several Can Do Canines graduating ceremonies; he was "blown away" by the stories he heard of what the dogs did for people and the ways that having an assistance dog had changed people's lives. Not only the person with a disability benefited, but the people around them did too. That was good news to Len. He knew it was stressful for his partner to never know when she would walk in to find him unconscious again. Furthermore when Len's blood sugar was low, he could get quite crabby. He wanted better for her and for himself. It was time for Len to apply for a Can Do Canines Diabetes Assist Dog.

He has had Rogue, a standard French poodle, for five years now. Even after hearing so many stories of praise for assistance dogs, he was not prepared for how profound an improvement Rogue would bring to his life. She has brought him deep peace of mind.

In Len's lifetime there have been great advances in technology for people with diabetes, and he has taken advantage of them. Rogue is better than all of them.

Rogue knows when Len's blood sugar is about to start dropping and that it is dangerous. She alerts him by nudging his stomach with her nose. If he takes no action and it continues to drop, she nudges him with more insistence. If he still takes no action, she will sit in front of him and vocalize. She does not bark. It is more like she is giving him a good "talking to." She will continue to nag him vocally until he makes a move to remedy the situation.

It took Len a while to realize just how accurate Rogue was. Early in their partnership, he would check his blood sugar when she nudged him, see that it was, for example, one hundred and forty (70 to 180 are normal ranges per Web MD[1]), and think to himself, "That's not bad. I'll just keep an eye on it." Except once his blood sugar starts to drop, it can plummet. Rogue did not like the "I'll just keep an eye on it" approach! She would stay extraordinarily focused on him, nudging him at the smallest change. It only took a couple times of not heeding her warnings for him to learn to trust her absolutely. Now when she nudges him, he does not wait, he does not question, he simply takes action. "The nose knows!"

Life is not all work though—one of Rogue's favorite times is when she gets to play with Len's baseball cap. Play time is also important bonding time and allows Rogue to destress from working all the time. Although she has time out of her vest, dog noses do not have an "off" switch.

Rogue is a tall, stately, black, standard French poodle wearing a red assistance dog vest. People notice her. Many of those people want to know more about her, so Len has become an outgoing and willing educator. He had suspected that having an assistance dog would bring him more into the public arena and he was right. He says that, since Rogue, what used to be a twenty-minute trip to the grocery store can now be up to an hour and a half, depending on how much educating he has to do! He will educate people about assistance dogs in general and about the correct way to act around an assistance dog. He will talk about standard poodles as assistance dogs, about diabetes assistance dogs, and about legitimate assistance dogs versus "fake" assistance dogs.

Len says it is easy to discern a real assistance dog from a fake one—just look at the behavior of the dog. Service dogs are calm but alert. They are focused on their handler and they do not concern themselves with others. They are well-behaved. They do not bark at people, squirrels, or other dogs. On the other hand, while some fake assistance dogs may be calm, they typically do not have the single-minded focus on their handlers that trained assistance dogs do. They may bark, growl, or wander to sniff at people or things. Once you have known a true assistance dog, the fake ones are easy to spot.

Once, Len had reservations at a hotel in Illinois. When he arrived, the manager wondered if Len could answer a question for him. Some time ago, guests had arrived with a dog that was wearing a service dog vest. They'd left the dog in the room, in a crate, while they went to a wedding. The dog barked and whined the entire time they were gone, which was most of the day. What could the distressed manager have done? Len told him, "Call the police. The dog has to go." That was not the behavior of a trained assistance dog, nor was it the behavior of an assistance dog owner because service dog owners receive training too.

Then the manager asked Len how his employees should handle any assistance dog situation. Is there a way to tell if it's a fake assistance dog?

Len told the manager what his options were when it came to identifying service dogs, by quoting the Americans with Disabilities Act: "When it is not obvious what service an animal provides, only limited inquiries are allowed. Staff may ask two questions: is the dog a service animal required because of a disability; and what work or task has the dog been trained to perform. Staff cannot ask about the person's disability, require medical documentation, require a special identification card or training documentation for the dog, or ask that the dog demonstrate its ability to perform the work or task."[2] In fact, people ask

Len about the proper protocol so often, that he carries copies of the law with him.

Fake service dogs can be irritating, but they can also be dangerous. Len and Rogue were walking in a park when he heard a commotion behind him and turned to see a pit-bull-type dog in a service dog vest (the type from the internet) charging toward Rogue. Thankfully, the owner managed to get the dog under control before anyone was hurt. Len and Rogue left the park, shaken but unharmed.

The vast majority of people Len and Rogue meet when they are out and about are respectful. They may be curious about assistance dogs. A woman once approached him to say she was a breeder of standard French poodles. She had not known they were used as assistance dogs. She thought she might want to donate a puppy to Can Do Canines, and she wondered if Len could tell her who to contact. He could and did. Since then, she has donated three puppies to Can Do Canines.

Len likes to visit antique shops and travels a lot to do so, with Rogue by his side. There was an occasion when a proprietor of an antique store saw Rogue and physically blocked Len from entering the store. Another teaching moment! Other than that one time, no one has questioned Rogue's right to be in an antique shop with Len. When visiting stores, Rogue is always perfectly behaved. Somehow, she knows that an antique store is no place to wag her tail! They have been in many shops and she has never disturbed any merchandise.

Len is unequivocal—having Rogue in his life has been nothing less than amazing.

References

1. "Normal Blood Sugar Levels for Adults With Diabetes," WebMD, accessed May 6, 2022, https://www.webmd.com/diabetes/normal-blood-sugar-levels-chart-adults

2. "ADA Requirements: Service Animals," ADA.gov, accessed May 6, 2022, https://www.ada.gov/service_animals_2010.htm

Chapter 11

GLENICE and YATES

"Sometimes God knows what you need."

Glenice first learned about hearing assistance dogs on a local news story, then a Google search led her to Can Do Canines. Coincidentally, her husband golfed with a man who fostered dogs for Can Do Canines. He showed her pictures of the dogs he had fostered over the years and encouraged her to apply for a Hearing Assist Dog, so she proceeded to apply. She received Yates, a black Labrador retriever, a year and a half ago when he was almost three years old.

Glenice was initially paired with a different dog—a much smaller dog. Glenice told me that being an assistance dog can be a stressful job for a dog. They are always on alert, paying attention to their handler, and paying attention to the world around them. The first dog did not easily recover from the daily stress of working, so it was returned to Can Do Canines. Glenice was then paired with Yates.

As a child, Glenice had pet dogs, but her husband had never had pets. Given that the first dog did not work out, there were some feelings of trepidation in the household before Yates came home. When he did arrive, he was much bigger than Glenice really wanted, but he was so friendly and kind that she fell in love with him immediately. After meeting him, his size was not an issue for her.

A Can Do Canines coach worked with Glenice and Yates in the home and out around town. They trained

Yates to alert Glenice to the sounds of a phone, a doorbell or door knock, a smoke alarm, and a kitchen timer.

Glenice has two cochlear implants, so she can often, but not always, hear those sounds. Sometimes she will feign deafness for Yates's sake, to keep him busy working and to keep his skills sharp. She does not wear her "ears" (cochlear implants) at night. "My nights are silent. Yates is my protector. I know he'll alert me when he hears the phone, or the smoke alarm, or the alarm clock." There are other things she does not hear, such as the time she was shopping and dropped her keys. She did not hear them hit the floor, so Yates nudged her. She responded to his nudge with "Show me." and he brought her over to the keys on the floor. Other times he will just pick up whatever she has dropped and bring it to her.

While he is happy to retrieve dropped items, he has absolutely no interest in playing fetch, which is unusual for a retriever breed. Glenice muses, "He knows he's got more important things to do." What he does love is to play hide and seek with his toys. Glenice will hide one of his toys and then tell him to find it. That is great fun for both of them and a game they play often.

Yates also enjoys cuddling. At Can Do Canines, the young dogs are trained to stay off the furniture. Glenice discovered very early that Yates likes to be right next to her, in contact with her; therefore, she says, "He gets to be on the furniture in my home." When he has his cape on and they are out of the house, he lines up right next to her leg, which she finds supportive and comforting.

Glenice's husband travels for work and is sometimes away overnight. Before Yates, Glenice was uncomfortable taking her "ears" off at night, yet she had to for comfort and health. Without them, there was no way she would know if the smoke alarm blared or if the phone rang. It was an anxious time for her, but now with Yates, she rests easy. It is the same when she visits her elderly parents in South Dakota. With Yates, she does not worry that she will not hear them if they need her at night—if someone were to fall or to call out, Yates would wake her. They now are training Yates to recognize her name, so if someone does call out her name, he will alert her. He is also learning to find her when her husband or daughter says, "Go get Glenny." He will go find her and nudge her, then she will say, "Show me." and he will take her to the person who needs her. A Can Do Canines coach helps Glenice with all the additional training she wants to do.

One unanticipated effect of having Yates took some time for Glenice to adjust to. Hearing loss is not a visible disability—Glenice says you can get through life without people knowing you have a disability. With cochlear implants, which she can cover with her hair, and along with reading lips, she could get by without people knowing she could not hear, but when she is with Yates, a big black dog wearing a red cape, people definitely know she has a disability. At first, she did not like having her disability be so visible. It took a while for her to get comfortable with that, but the benefits of having a Hearing Assist Dog far outweighed any nervousness about being visible.

As you might imagine, for someone who relies on reading lips, the face masks used during the COVID pandemic are a big problem. When Glenice would walk into a store and see people's faces covered, her anxiety would spike. However with Yates at her side, it is clear to others that she has some kind of special need, so they are more open to helping her. Glenice reports, "If I tell people that I read lips, they'll more readily pull their mask down. They see Yates and they know." Yates has been a tremendous comfort in these trying times of COVID.

Glenice's family has a lake cabin which, before Yates, she would not go to alone. Now she and Yates are happy to go there, although that took a bit of training for Yates. The cabin is at the top of a steep hill and at first Yates did not want to climb that hill. Glenice consulted with a Can Do Canine's coach and learned how to approach the problem in small steps. Glenice and Yates worked through it and now he does not give the hill a second thought. The process of working though that problem has increased their trust and confidence in one another.

When she was home alone, Glenice's husband would always worry about her. Now, because of Yates, he is free from that worry. Her daughters used to be concerned that she would not be able to hear a car approaching when she was walking in a parking lot because there had been times when they had been with her that they had to say, "Mom, wait! There's a car coming." Now they are confident that although she may miss a sound, Yates will not. Glenice is safe and the entire family feels relieved.

Having Yates has been a positive experience for Glenice and her family, and she would encourage others, even if they feel like it might be a daunting thing to have an assistance dog, to go ahead and do it. For her, it was not an easy decision to make. Not having a pet since childhood, she was not sure if she could do it. Besides, taking a dog into public places was not something she ever dreamed she would do. Glenice has this to say to those who are thinking about having an assistance dog, "Even though it's a big unknown, you won't be alone. Can Do Canines and Can Do graduates will educate you and help you find your way."

Helping others find their way is something Glenice does for people who are new to cochlear implants. Getting a cochlear implant is not the same experience for everyone. For example, some people will be able to hear music, but others will not. So much depends on when a person lost their hearing; someone who lost hearing late in life, like Glenice, has a memory of sound, a memory of music. The younger a person is when they lose their hearing, the less memory their brain has for recall. In a program called Hearing Journey,[1] Glenice guides people through the experience of getting cochlear implants and she also has a blog about cochlear implants. You can find her blog, *2 Bionic Ears,* at https://2bionicears.wordpress.com/

References

1. Hearing Journey
   https://www.hearingjourney.com

Chapter 12

RIDGE and PEGGY

"With Peggy, I'm able to live my life."

In the summer of 1997, Ridge was living in Arizona. One day, as he was mowing the lawn, he got a very bad headache. Going inside, he drank some water and tried to nap, hoping the headache would be gone when he woke up, but it only got worse. By evening he was slurring his words and having trouble with his balance; fearing he was having a stroke, his girlfriend took him to the hospital. Twenty-four hours later, he was completely "locked-in"—he could see and hear but was completely paralyzed except for his eyes—he could blink his eyes but could not move his body or make any sounds. He was in that state for three months and was eventually diagnosed with both meningitis and encephalitis.

Recovery was extremely slow. It started with the ability to make sounds. The entire time he was locked-in, he had focused on trying to move his big toe and then, not long after his voice came back, he moved it. Oh, he was excited! His mother and girlfriend were with him, as they were every morning, and he wanted to shout "Hurrah!" and let them know. Unfortunately although he could make noises, he was not yet able to form words. They all could tell though that whatever was happening was a very good thing!

Recovering was a long and arduous journey of re-learning to talk, to walk, to eat, to get dressed, to take care of himself—everything. He moved back to Minnesota, where he found a dog at the local shelter (he was an experienced dog trainer) and trained it to be his assistance dog. He went on to train two other dogs to be his assistance dogs after the first one. This time when he needed a dog, his vision and hearing had diminished too much for him to be able to train another dog. He applied to Can Do Canines, was accepted, and was paired with Peggy, a lovely black Labrador retriever.

The first time Peggy saw him, she got quite excited and started to run to him. The trainer called her back and she went to him at a more sedate pace, but it was clear from that first glance that she knew he was for her—and he knew she was for him. They have been together now for almost three years.

Peggy is multi-talented. She is both a Hearing Assist Dog and a Mobility Assist Dog. When they are walking, she is his guide. Her help is especially important at curbs and other changes in elevation, which cause Ridge to fall. If there is one, she will find the curb cut for him. Ridge drops things; Peggy is always happy to pick them up. She alerts him to sounds such as the phone, the oven timer, and the doorbell. In fact, whenever someone is at the door, she barks—the only time she ever barks. She helps him get dressed in the morning by bringing his leg braces to him and she helps him get undressed at bedtime. She is so focused on him that he often does not have to tell her what he needs from her; she sees it and is right there, helping.

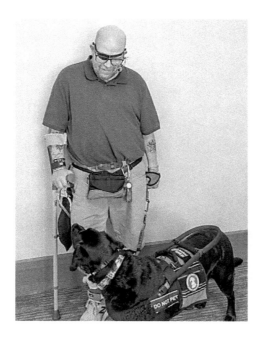

As to how they were coping with the COVID pandemic restrictions, Ridge said they get out of the apartment frequently, for example, he makes three trips to his doctors every week. He joked that going to the doctor was his part time job! Even though they go out, Peggy misses playing with her dog friends. They do not go to a dog park, as she is too important to risk her getting hurt or sick there. Ridge has friends who have three dogs, and before COVID, he and Peggy would go there often; he would take Peggy's harness off so she could play with the dogs. She would play and he could visit with his friends. Everyone misses those visits and they are all hoping before too long that they will be able to get together again.

Ridge's love for Peggy is evident in how well he takes care of her, making sure she is healthy inside and out. He does not know what he would do without her. He says, "With Peggy, I'm able to live my life. I can't imagine being without her."

Ridge has this to say to people thinking about getting an assistance dog; they take a lot of work, even more so than a pet dog. Assistance dogs are working full-time, so they must get the best of everything—the best food, grooming, exercise, and veterinary care—the very best life. They give you your best life; you must do the same for them. If you are sure you are ready to commit to care for an assistance dog then do it. The improvement in your life will be amazing.

There's one more thing Ridge would like to say, and that is that he is transgender (trans). People with disabilities are often seen as only that—someone with a disability, but they are also many other things. They are mothers and fathers, wives and husbands, artists and lawyers, scientists and musicians, executives and workers. They are men and women, queer and straight, gay and lesbian, trans. They are everything and they also can have a disability. Their disability may be all you know about them, but it is not all there is to know.

Chapter 13

TERRI and PEACHES

"Peaches is pure joy to me. I'm so lucky to have her."

Peaches is Terri's second dog trained as both a Seizure Assist Dog and Mobility Assist Dog from Can Do Canines Assistance Dogs in Minnesota. Peaches is also a Hearing Assist Dog. Terri's previous Seizure Assist Dog and Mobility Assist Dog, Brody, also a black Labrador retriever, was with her for eleven and a half years. An in-depth story about Terri and Brody is in another book on assistance dogs, *Doctor Dogs* by Maria Goodavage.[1] Peaches, on the other hand, has only been with Terri for a few months, with training ongoing. Regardless of how young and inexperienced Peaches is, she does remarkable work for Terri, especially as a Seizure Assist Dog. As Terri says, *"She is a fast study."*

When she was twenty-seven, Terri was a police officer in Louisiana. She was injured in an explosion while working and suffered a brain injury. That was the beginning of her life with tonic-clonic (formerly known as grand mal) seizures.

To help control her seizures, Terri has a Vagus Nerve Stimulator (VNS) implanted in her chest. It delivers a mild electrical impulse to the vagus nerve every five minutes, which then stimulates the part of the brain where seizures originate. It does not completely prevent seizures, but it does limit their duration to five minutes. There is also a special magnet she can use to activate the device when she knows a seizure is about to happen which will then help prevent the seizure. Terri carries the magnet and she need only brush her chest with it to activate the VNS. In Terri's case, however, she has absolutely no warning that a seizure is imminent, leaving no time to touch her chest with the magnet. The magnet is essentially useless to her—when she is alone, that is.

Terri may have no way of knowing that a seizure is about to occur, but Peaches knows—and Peaches is always with her. When Peaches senses that a seizure is coming, she will alert Terri by nudging her leg, or if they are in a crowded environment such as a shopping mall, she will bark twice. Terri then has time to get down to the ground because when a seizure comes, Terri collapses, unconscious. If she happens to be somewhere dangerous, say on steps or crossing a street, it can be big trouble. Terri has had too many traumatic brain injuries, broken bones, and surgeries to be able to correct all of the injuries she has sustained from falling during seizures.

Once Peaches alerts her and she gets down, she will command Peaches, *"Snuggle!"* Peaches wears one of Terri's magnets on her collar, and at the command to snuggle, she will press herself onto Terri's chest to activate the VNS. Terri and Lora, her life partner, fondly and humorously refer to this as Peaches "zapping" Terri. Peaches will lie with Terri until it is clear that the device has worked and no other seizure is on its way. Often, Terri is in her motorized wheelchair when Peaches alerts her. In that case, she will be sure she is belted in and then give

Peaches the command to snuggle. Peaches will rise up so she can press against Terri's chest, then she will stay in contact with Terri until it is safe to sit down beside her.

Terri and Peaches practice "snuggling"

Terri and Lora had a beloved pet Rottweiler before Brody, named Isabeaux, or Izzy. She was not a trained assistance dog, but she knew how to comfort Terri, particularly after a seizure. Izzy would lie by her and lick her hands and face, which helped Terri as she regained consciousness. Since Lora worked, Terri felt safer with Izzy near her. When Izzy eventually died from bone cancer, Terri did not know how she could go on, suffering through multiple seizures a week, without Izzy for comfort. Then her neurologist told her there were seizure assistance dogs. She quickly started looking online for information about assistance dogs and found an organization, Can Do Canines Assistance Dogs, which was actually located quite near to where Terri lived. Then she forgot that she had been doing that research—too many brain injuries have affected her memory. Thankfully, Lora did not forget. She followed up with Can Do Canines, calling them and sending in the application. She did not tell Terri about what she had done until a trainer from Can Do Canines called to schedule a visit in their home. Terri was delighted that Lora had remembered and applied! Can Do Canines approved the application and soon Terri was partnered with Brody.

It was while Brody was her Seizure Assist Dog partner that she had the idea he could be taught to somehow use the VNS magnet. Before that, Brody would alert Terri, she would get down in a safe place, and Brody, who weighed over ninety pounds, would lie on her until the seizure passed. He could help her be safe during a seizure, but he could not help prevent them. Terri talked to the trainer at Can Do Canines, who agreed it was a good idea to teach Brody to use the VNS. Brody easily learned to use the magnet attached to his collar, and the number of seizures Terri experienced greatly decreased. In 2014, Brody was named Service Dog of the Year by the Minnesota Veterinary Medical Association as the first service dog to ever learn to activate the VNS.

Brody saved Terri's life many times and they did not all have to do with seizures. There was a time when Brody became very interested in Terri's neck, nuzzling and licking it. It confused her since it was unusual behavior for him. When it became painful, she went to her doctor and learned she had thyroid cancer. Her doctor told her that the cancer was detected far earlier than is typical. She knew she had Brody to thank for that.

Terri also has a pacemaker for her heart. Brody would alert her when heart rhythm was abnormal by blocking her way. No one taught it to him—it was something he picked up on his own.

Peaches, who Terri calls "home grown" since she was bred for Can Do Canines, shows every sign of being as talented as Brody was. Terri says, "She's already ninety-five percent there, and we've really just started."

One important benefit Terri gets from having an assistance dog is visibility. People tell her, "You don't look like there is anything wrong with you." Terri has several disabilities and not all of them are visible to the casual observer, but all of them do affect her ability to operate in the world every day. Peaches not only provides the essential and life-saving help Terri needs, but her presence makes it clear to others that Terri is a person with a disability, relieving Terri of the need to explain herself to strangers.

Terri and Peaches are members of the self-named Grad Pack. This group of five handlers and dogs, all graduates of Can Do Canines, gets together regularly. The dogs play together in back yards; the group visits shopping malls and restaurants; and once a month, they gather at Terri's, where a mobile groomer pampers all of the dogs. The Grad Pack provides valuable support to all the members besides being lots of fun for both the handlers and the dogs.

Terri took a break from the Grad Pack when she first got Peaches. She also took a break from all the public speaking she'd been doing for Can Do Canines. In addition to speaking for Can Do Canines, for several years Terri and a friend—a Minneapolis firefighter—trained Minneapolis police and emergency responders about assistance dogs, including the federal and state laws pertaining to them. She took a break from all of it to devote her time to Peaches. It was essential that they bond, and she wanted to be sure that Peaches was happy to "zap" her with the magnet when necessary. "I needed to be sure that I'd taught her well enough so she knows what to do when I'm unconscious." Peaches knows. Now Terri can resume her activities as a public speaker for Can Do Canines.

From feeling hopeless when Izzy died, to living a satisfying life, Terri is amazed at what Brody and now Peaches have given her. There is no question that Peaches is devoted to Terri; they have a loving and caring partnership. Every day Terri experiences profound gratitude for having Peaches in her life. Not only Terri is grateful—Lora rests easy knowing that Peaches is with Terri and will always take good care of her.

References

1. Maria Goodavage, *Doctor Dogs: How Our Best Friends Are Becoming Our Best Medicine.* (New York: Dutton, 2019), 71-82.

Chapter 14

COLLEEN and ELSA

"Elsa is the best helper in the whole world."

olleen and Elsa have been together eight years. Elsa is an eleven-year-old black Labrador retriever—a Hearing Assist Dog. When Colleen first started talking with me about Elsa, she became teary eyed but said they were happy tears, tears of love. Elsa's dedication to Colleen's well-being is obvious to see; just as obvious, Elsa means the world to Colleen. They are bonded in service and in love. Service is Elsa's life work, and service is an essential part of Colleen's life. Colleen volunteers as much and as often as she can with Elsa ever-present at her side.

Let's go back to their beginning.

Colleen looked after her ailing husband until his death. After he died, Colleen had the idea of trying a hearing assistance dog. Since she was then living alone, she would have help to hear the phone, doorbell, oven timer, alarm clock, and other household sounds. When she was outside, she would have someone to alert her to traffic and to people who were approaching from the side or rear. She applied to Can Do Canines, a nonprofit Minnesota assistance dog training organization.

Elsa was originally trained as a Mobility Assist Dog by Can Do Canines. After Colleen applied, the Can Do Canine trainers decided to add to Elsa's training so she could also be a Hearing Assist Dog. When Elsa hears something Colleen needs to know, she makes physical contact with Colleen, then leads her to the sound. Since Colleen is hearing impaired and is fluent in American Sign Language, Elsa became bi-lingual. She not only understands English but she understands American Sign Language! Here Colleen is signing "sit" to Elsa.

Colleen signing "sit"

Although hearing assistance is Elsa's primary duty, her mobility training has been put to good use also. Colleen worked as an administrative assistant in a large business, and she took the bus to and from work, with Elsa to help on those daily trips. One of Colleen's duties at work was delivering mail throughout the company. Elsa accompanied her on all her rounds. Colleen is a good-natured, cheerful, and friendly person, and she laughs as she says that Elsa was more popular than she was. Everyone looked forward to the mail delivery so they could say hello to Elsa.

When Colleen needed a hip replacement, Elsa's mobility training became an essential part of her work for Colleen. It was a blessing to Colleen to have her dear friend Elsa help her in new and necessary ways. Since Colleen could not bend over, Elsa would pick things up that she dropped; she could get things that were kept on low shelves or in low cupboards; and she could even help Colleen get dressed and undressed. One morning, not long after her hip surgery, Colleen's sister stopped by to see how she was doing and to help her get dressed. You can imagine her surprise when she found Colleen dressed and ready for the day. Colleen laughs at the memory. She and Elsa were both quite proud of what they had accomplished that day. Now, even though Colleen can do it herself, she still lets Elsa take her socks off—Elsa loves helping Colleen.

After Colleen retired, she volunteered in a hospital gift shop. She says Elsa was good for business, because people would see Elsa through the window and go into the shop hoping to visit with her. Often, they would end up purchasing something. Then the COVID pandemic restrictions closed the gift shop. Both Colleen and Elsa miss that work, but as COVID restrictions have begun to lift, Colleen is actively looking for other volunteer opportunities. Colleen loves to be of service to the community, and Elsa loves to be of service to Colleen.

Chapter 15

LEVI and DEMPSEY

"I have physical limitations, and so does my service dog. But we are still able to be contributing members of society. We are still of value."

D empsey is named after Clint Dempsey, a professional soccer player who underwent two heart surgeries before he retired in 2018. That fact is pertinent because Dempsey the assistance dog, recently had heart surgery too.

Levi had noticed that Dempsey was not his usual energetic and happy self, so they went to see the veterinarian. After a series of tests, Dempsey was diagnosed with a third degree (the most severe) atrioventricular block, which was putting stress on his heart and causing it to beat improperly. On the day after his fifth birthday, Dempsey, the dog, went into surgery to have a pacemaker installed. At the time of our interview, Dempsey was still recovering and was not yet back to working full time. Like people with a medical condition, Dempsey now wears a medical identification tag.

Dempsey is Levi's first Mobility Assist Dog. Levi knew about assistance dogs, but he thought he did not really need one. He told himself that there were so many people who had more of a need than he did. As time passed, he began to notice that he was having more difficulty in his day-to-day life. Coincidentally, around that time, the company he worked for held a Disability Awareness Fair. Levi volunteered to help at the fair and there he met someone with an assistance dog who was representing Can Do Canines, a Minnesota assistance dog training organization. They talked and Levi started thinking more seriously about getting an assistance dog. He decided to apply, assuming that there would be a twelve- to eighteen-month wait and thinking by then he would probably be ready for a dog. He applied in November. Much to his surprise, three months later he was teamed with Dempsey.

Dempsey was the first and only assistance dog he met at Can Do Canines. Levi says it was love at first sight—as though they immediately recognized one another. Those magical moments are due to the intensive preparation and planning of the staff at Can Do Canines. They asked Levi all about his life—what his average day was like; where he lived, worked, and shopped; how he got to and from various places; who his friends were; what he liked to do for entertainment and leisure activities—until they had a clear picture of Levi's life. With that information they knew just how a Mobility Assist Dog could be useful to him. They also asked Levi how he thought a Mobility Assist Dog could help him. At the time, Levi was working eight hours a day and commuting on the train over an hour each way. One thing Levi knew for sure was he needed a dog with a lot of stamina.

Now, because of COVID pandemic restrictions, Levi is working much less and his current job is walking distance from home. His days are considerably less active than before, which fits perfectly with Dempsey's need for some recovery time. Dempsey is expected to fully recover all his vim and vigor and Levi hopes that the loosening of COVID restrictions will coincide with their increased activity—because Dempsey is all about being active! He is always ready for adventure, always ready to say, "Hey! Let's go do something! Let's play ball!" Even though he's an eager and energetic dog, he has accepted his need for recovery time's slower pace. Levi has worked hard to keep Dempsey calm while at the same time letting him work enough to keep him happy and his skills sharp. So far it has gone well. Levi says, "I'm determined to take good care of him, just as he takes good care of me."

Dempsey was trained to do many things, and at the beginning of their partnership, Levi had to learn all the commands Dempsey knew so they could communicate using the same language. Levi asks, "Did you know that service dogs are trained to go potty on command?" That is just one of Dempsey's special skills! Dempsey was trained to pick up dropped items, but he had to figure out on his own how to pick up a credit card from a smooth tile floor when Levi dropped one. It was tricky, but he persisted and he got it. They had a happy celebration with lots of applause. "Bravo! You did it! Good work!" Now Dempsey can pick up anything.

Dempsey is glad when he's given a task. When Levi tells him to get the phone, he runs to the phone, and runs with the phone back to Levi, tail wagging all the while. He also helps with doors. He will either press the automatic door button, or if there is not one, he will use his body to help Levi open the door. He lifts spirits as well. Levi says, "He gives me a reason to get out of bed every morning. He helps me stay engaged with the world, especially now, during COVID, when isolating would be so easy. He forces me to not be so closed off." One way Levi stays engaged with the world is to stop at his favorite neighborhood coffee shop every morning, and while people might be shy of attempting to interact with a person in a wheelchair, Dempsey is an icebreaker. People happily catch Levi's eye and wish him a good morning.

Levi lives in the downtown area of a large metropolitan city. He says he is fortunate to live in a city where there is a high level of awareness about assistance dogs and the rights of people with disabilities. He has never been refused service at a restaurant or any other place because Dempsey is with him. Most of the people he sees on the street know better than to try and engage Dempsey's attention. Although a couple of times, young children have run up to Dempsey and hugged him before anyone could stop them. Dempsey just turns to look at Levi, as if to say,

"Dude. This kid is hugging me. Does this kid not know that I am working?" With a rush of fondness, Levi sends an answering thought, *"I know, my friend, I know. I'll take care of it."* Then he turns to the child and the attending adults. "Can I tell you about my dog? See that red thing he's wearing? That's called a cape, a service dog cape, and it has a very special meaning..."

The cost is forty thousand dollars or more to breed and train a service dog. Levi is grateful to have Dempsey, and he's glad to give back in any way he can. Not only to Can Do Canines, but to the wider assistance dog community. When he first got Dempsey, if Levi had any questions about life with an assistance dog, he turned to other Can Do Canines graduates for information and support. Now, after three years partnered with Dempsey, Levi, on social media, serves as a coach for newer Can Do Canine graduates. That way, people can reach out to someone who has actually experienced what they are wondering about. "Going to a hotel? Okay, here's what you need to know." Levi's commitment to giving back is why he agreed to be interviewed, why he is glad to talk with people on the street, and why he does public speaking about service dogs to a variety of organizations. Levi is glad to be of service.

Dempsey loves being of service, too. You can see it in the way he walks and holds himself when he has his assistance dog cape on. Levi says if we could understand what he says to other dogs, it would be, "Check it out! I'm a working dog! Do you do this for your human?"

Chapter 16

LINDSEY and COOKIE

"Cookie is an angel."

Lindsey has worn hearing aids since she was two years old. When she moved out of her childhood home and into an apartment with another deaf person, her mother encouraged her to apply for a Hearing Assist Dog from Can Do Canines, an assistance dog training organization in Minnesota. Lindsey's family always had dogs when she was growing up, so she resonated with the idea of having an assistance dog. She applied.

Her first Hearing Assist Dog from Can Do Canines was Roscoe. Lindsey and Roscoe were in training with a Can Do Canines coach for a year and a half. When it was time for her to get her second Hearing Assist Dog, Cookie, Can Do Canines had revamped their training system, so they only trained for six months. For the "public access" part of the training, Lindsey would meet with Cookie and the trainer at a shopping mall, or airport, or restaurant, or even a busy downtown street. The rest of the training was done at Lindsey's home. That was all six years ago, when Cookie was two, which makes Cookie eight years old now.

Although Lindsey lived in that apartment for eleven years, it was beginning to feel more and more cramped. Then she got married to Michael. So she, and he, and Cookie, now live in a large apartment in the basement of a house owned by one of her former roommates. They have their own entrance and use of the back yard. The back yard makes a big difference to Cookie, who gets plenty of play time there. It matters to Lindsey, too—now there is no need to go for nighttime walks, which were a challenge due to her decreasing vision.

Cookie was trained to alert Lindsey to sounds. Cookie even has a favorite sound—the oven timer! Lindsey says Cookie loves that sound! Cookie also alerts if someone is near the house, and while storms and fireworks don't disturb Cookie, she alerts Lindsey when they are close.

One day at their lake cabin, Lindsey and her husband, Michael, who also has a hearing impairment, forgot to turn on the septic tank pump. An alarm blared, although neither of them could hear it. Cookie alerted them, they followed her, and then they could literally feel the alarm vibrations. Cookie had not been trained for anything at the cabin because she is off duty there. The lake is considered her free time, and even though she is not officially on duty, on some level she is always doing her job.

There are many differences between Lindsey's former Hearing Assist Dog, Roscoe, and Cookie. Some of those differences show up at the cabin. Roscoe was wild about squirrels and chased them at every chance. Cookie is unconcerned about squirrels, but she loves the water. Not so much being in the water, but being on it. Lindsey has a standup paddleboard, and Cookie loves riding on it—likewise the kayak. Although she can swim—she is a black Labrador, after all—she always wears a life jacket. She also likes to relax on the pontoon boat. One thing she is not interested in is speed boats. Speed is not her thing.

Although she likes being out in nature, Cookie definitely does not like camping. She likes boating, she likes hiking the trails, but she does not like mosquitos, and she wants to sleep at home, not in a tent. In fact, she has her own futon at home, and if anyone sits on it, she gives them the "glare-eye look." You can almost hear her saying

"MOVE!" She does not use her futon at night, preferring to sleep on the bed with Lindsey and Michael. It is a king-size bed, but still it is crowded—Cookie is a big dog! Often, she will move in the night to sleep on the floor beside Lindsey's side of the bed. Cookie always stays close.

Lindsey's young nephew has learned from Cookie. When he was old enough to walk, but was not yet talking, he went to Lindsey and kept pointing to the kitchen. When Lindsey understood that he was alerting her to a sound, she took his hand and followed him. The refrigerator was beeping! The door was not closed all the way. He had so often seen Cookie do the same thing that he just naturally alerted Lindsey when he heard a sound. Smart.

Eight years ago, Lindsey began to lose her vision; she is now legally blind. She has almost no night vision, and crowded spaces are visually challenging. When her vision began to fail, she decided to get a cochlear implant on her right side, the worst side for her hearing. While it was very helpful, there were some aspects of having just one implant that were confusing. For example, no matter where a sound originated—on her left, or right, behind her, or above her—she always heard it in her right ear, as if coming from the right side. A few months ago, with Michael's encouragement, she got a cochlear implant on the left side as well. The second implant has made a huge difference in perceiving sounds. She loves it and is very glad she did it. The new implant has new technology, such as Bluetooth, which definitely has been a learning curve for her, but she is getting used to it.

For her decreasing vision, the other thing Lindsey did was train Cookie to alert her to curbs when they are walking. Cookie was trained as a Hearing Assist Dog and is not really a guide dog, but she is a smart dog and she is learning new ways to help Lindsey.

As with everyone with an assistance dog, Lindsey is concerned about people who bring their emotional support dogs into stores. Too often, according to Lindsey, when those dogs see Cookie, they "yip yap, and they keep yip yapping," distracting Cookie and Lindsey both. Cookie does not bark, but other people will sometimes glare at Lindsey, as though the disturbance was her fault.

Those yippy dogs give true assistance dogs a bad name. It is very frustrating for Lindsey. For the same reason, Lindsey does not like to go to pet-friendly stores. Cookie is always well-behaved, but other dogs bark at her, and many owners do nothing to make them behave.

To people who are thinking about getting an assistance dog, Lindsey warned they should be prepared for all of the initial training, and for continuing the training for the duration of the partnership. Otherwise, she said, "Have fun." Keep trying new things with your dog— some will work, some will not: like Cookie, who loves walking on trails, but hates camping. Cookie enjoys kayaking, but some dogs will not get into a kayak or a canoe. Reach out to your trainer and other people with assistance dogs if you have any questions. Participate in Can Do Canine activities when you can, like the weekly walk in the mall sponsored by Can Do Canine trainers. Lindsey is unable to participate in that activity because she works during the day, although she would if she could. She works four days a week in a warehouse, in receiving and shipping. In a five-hour shift, she walks over nine thousand steps. That's too much for Cookie, especially as she is getting older, so she stays home.

Besides her job, and boating and kayaking at the cabin whenever she can, Lindsey teaches protactile. She teaches interpreters and she teaches people who are deafblind. In fact, she is President of the Minnesota DeafBlind Association.

If you have not heard of protactile, here is a brief description from Wikipedia:

> *Protactile is a language used by deafblind people using tactile channels. Unlike other sign languages, which are heavily reliant on visual information, protactile is oriented toward touch and is practiced on the body. Protactile communication originated out of communications by deafblind people in Seattle in 2007, and incorporates signs from American Sign Language. Protactile is an emerging system of communication in the United States, with users relying on shared principles such as contact space, tactile imagery, and reciprocity.*[1]

Much more information on protactile can be found in a *New Yorker* article by Andrew Leland: "Deafblind Communities May Be Creating a New Language of Touch."[2]

Lindsey also teaches technology to people who are deafblind, such as how to use an iPad, iPhone, or computer.

As you can tell, helping people is an important value for Lindsey. She and Cookie regularly visit older people who are deafblind, helping them with various household tasks and providing companionship. Lindsey enjoys these interactions very much and of one person, in particular, she says, "She's my third grandma."

Cookie certainly shares Lindsey's willingness to help. Trained to alert only Lindsey, she will also alert Michael, and when they visit Lindsey's mother, Cookie will alert her too. She watches over the whole family. Lindsey says, "Cookie is an angel" —a guardian angel.

References

1. "Protactile," Wikipedia, accessed May 6, 2022, https://en.wikipedia.org/wiki/Protactile
2. Andrew Leland, "Deafblind Communities May Be Creating a New Language of Touch." *New Yorker*, accessed May 12, 2022, https://www.newyorker.com/culture/annals-of-inquiry/deafblind-communities-may-be-creating-a-new-language-of-touch.

Chapter 17

MIKE and ELLIE

*"Can Do Canines gave me this bundle of joy.
I am forever grateful."*

Mike's cousin thought it would be great if Mike had an assistance dog. He agreed, so she helped him find one. Born with cerebral palsy, Mike does not have the use of his left hand, and he has had so many surgeries on his left foot that his mobility is limited. He thought a Mobility Assist Dog would be helpful in many ways, but Ellie, a yellow Labrador retriever from Can Do Canines, has been a bigger help than he ever dreamed possible. They have been together for two years.

Mike suffers from extreme shyness, a result of the bullying he experienced throughout his school years. Ellie is changing that—being in public with her forces him to interact with people. As he has grown more comfortable, he is happy to meet new people now. However, with more social activities comes Mike's pet peeve—the times that people, uninvited, try to talk to Ellie or even pet her, even though she is wearing her assistance dog cape. Mike would like people to know that the proper and safe assistance dog etiquette is to ignore Ellie completely. If you want to talk to her or pet her, first ask Mike; he may or may not say yes. It is not a simple thing to interact with an assistance dog. First Mike will have to be sure everyone is in a safe place—not blocking anyone's way and safe for Ellie—then he will have to remove Ellie's assistance dog cape so she knows she is free to interact with you. Only when he gives her the signal that it is okay, and he tells you it is okay, can you talk to her or pet her, whichever

Mike has designated. With respect and good will, you may make two new friends!

The Can Do Canines organization also plays an important role for Mike as he recovers from his shyness. Now that things are opening up after the COVID-19 pandemic lockdown, Can Do Canines is once again offering outings and Mike is so glad. He gets to meet and mingle with people—new friends—with whom he shares life experiences. Recently they toured a brewery, and while Mike does not drink alcohol, it was fun to socialize with the other Can Do Canine graduates. Another activity he participated in was the "Flight to Nowhere." The Can Do Canine group went to the airport, where they rode the tram, went through security, and then went to a room that had been set up like the passenger compartment of a plane. They got to practice the whole process, from arriving at the airport to being on the plane, with their assistance dogs and in one another's positive presence. Mike wonders where he would like to go on a plane!

Coming up soon is Can Do Canine's "Woof-a-Roo," an outdoor family-fun event that will include live music, a dog costume contest, dog centric vendors, dog demonstrations, concessions, prizes, and a one-mile walk.

Speaking of families, Mike has a large, extended one, and Ellie has been accepted as part of the family. She does not wear her assistance dog cape at family gatherings, so she gets to romp with the pet dogs and play ball with the children. All fun, except one time, when someone came with a dog that barked at Ellie relentlessly, until Mike and Ellie had to go indoors. Actually that worked to Mike's advantage because Mike's grandfather was also inside; Mike got to spend the day with him while everyone else played outside. His grandfather died a few weeks later, so even though it was irritating at the time, Mike is grateful to that misbehaving dog for giving him precious time with his grandfather.

While Ellie helps Mike with shyness, that is really a by-product of her primary job as Mike's Mobility Assist Dog. It is a job she is good at. One of her main duties is to pick up things that Mike has dropped. She gets things for him, like his phone or the TV remote, and she helps with dressing him by bringing him his shoes. She is quite handy too at helping him undress—removing his jacket, shirt, and socks. Mike uses a walking stick for balance, and she will get that for him if he drops it. She is a good shopper; she gets items from the shelves and brings them to him, and when they are done shopping, she will carry their purchases in a plastic bag, in her teeth!

If he falls, she is there. One way she helps if he falls is to brace herself so he can lean on her to get up. He cannot put all of his weight on her, but she helps steady him as he gets up. If he is unable to arise, she will press the medical alert button he wears.

Mike and Ellie are the seven hundred and first team to graduate from Can Do Canines. They trained with a Can Do Canine trainer at a large shopping mall. Besides learning to ignore people, they learned to navigate stairs, elevators, and crowds. They spent about seventeen hours there over a period of several days. Every time they went there, Mike noticed improvements in how he and Ellie worked together. Mike knows the training never stops; he carries treats wherever they go, so when Ellie does something particularly well, she gets a scrumptious treat!

Knowing how hard he and Ellie have worked to be a mobility assistance dog team, Mike wishes people would stop misrepresenting their pets and emotional support dogs as assistance dogs.

He does not disparage the bond people have with their pets; he has had pet dogs himself and he knows how important that bond can be to someone. The issue to him is that assistance dogs are specially trained—they go through a lengthy and rigorous training—and pets are not. Assistance dog handlers are trained as well, and pet owners are not. Far too often, a person claiming their pet is an assistance dog (with a vest from the internet), allows the dog act in ways that true assistance dogs never would act, thereby giving assistance dogs a bad reputation—perhaps the owner allows their dog to approach a passerby, or to take food someone offers, or to continue to bark, or to urinate or defecate in inappropriate areas. These would not be considered acceptable behaviors for a well-trained assistance dog.

Mike has exciting plans for the future. Currently he is preparing for a presentation at the local Lion's Club, where he will appear with a trainer from Can Do Canines. Speaking in front of a group is surely a challenge for him, but he really, really wants to do it. Ellie has helped Mike understand himself better; more than a shy person with a disability, he discovered he is an adventurer! He is someone willing and able to take risks.

Mike now lives with his father, but he is actively pursuing an apartment of his own. With Ellie, he is confident about living on his own. He wanted to do this interview in a park he had never been to before, "Don't worry, Ellie and I will find our way there!" He is also saving for a train trip; he is not sure where they will go, he and Ellie, but he wants the experience of riding on a train and staying in a sleeper car. Amtrak has special disability sleeper cars, which will make it easier to have Ellie with him. His trip will probably be short, maybe only overnight, but he is eager to try it. Then he has another idea he got from fellow Can Do Canine graduate—train Ellie to accompany him in a canoe! Yes, Mike has plenty of adventures coming up and Ellie will make all of them possible.

Mike would like to tell everyone with any kind of disability to look into getting an assistance dog. He hopes other people can experience the benefits and blessings of a partnership with an assistance dog.

Chapter 18

JOAN and FRANKIE

"Frankie's only two, and I already worry about what I'll do when she can no longer work. She's so helpful to me, I can't imagine how I'd get by without her."

Joan has always had dogs, and she has trained them for many things, for example when she owned a sheep ranch, she trained her dogs to herd sheep, a complex task indeed. Loving all animals, she was a veterinary technician for twenty years. It was natural then that she also became an "animal communicator," for instance—a racehorse trainer phoned her from New York. He had a horse that was underperforming, and he could not figure out why. Could she help? She communicated with the horse, intuitively and long distance, and learned that the horse was not getting much rest because he and the horse in the stall next to him did not like each other. There was constant tension when they were both in the stable. She suggested to the trainer that he find a way to separate them—to put as much distance between them as possible. He did so and the horse started winning races!

Suffice it to say, Joan has a lot of experience with animals. She also has narcolepsy—she can suddenly find herself falling asleep anytime, anywhere.

When Joan got divorced and moved to an apartment, she had to leave her herding dogs behind at the ranch. Still, she wanted a dog companion, so she got a West Highland white terrier (Westie). One thing she noticed about the Westie was that her attention was focused on any and all wildlife around her. That was very different from Joan's herding dogs, who had always paid close attention to her, ready and eager to follow her next command. Curious, she started to intently study the personality types and innate abilities of various dog breeds, which led her to think about the possibility of a narcolepsy assistance dog. Her children, along with her coworkers and friends, had learned to recognize the signs of an oncoming narcoleptic event so they could alert her to it. Joan knew her children would eventually leave the nest to go off and live their lives. She had to find more help before then.

Around this same time, her narcolepsy started getting worse. Her neurologist told her she could expect it to continue to get worse as she aged and that she would probably lose her driving privileges sooner rather than later. He prescribed medication. She practiced meditation. Both helped, but not enough. She definitely needed more help; she needed an assistance dog.

Joan researched as widely and as deeply as she could, looking for an organization that supplied narcolepsy assist dogs, or for someone who trained narcolepsy assist dogs, or for information about training one's own narcolepsy assistance dog, or just information about what breed of dog would be appropriate. She found nothing.

Narcolepsy is triggered by strong emotions—extreme happiness, depression, tension, exuberance, anxiety—any kind of stress. Joan was aware that some people had emotional support dogs, which seemed at least related to her emotions. So that became her starting point—she would find an emotional support dog and see what difference it made in her life. She knew the qualities she wanted in a support dog: It had to be highly intelligent; it would naturally focus on her; it must be calm but also alert; and it had to be highly intuitive. It was a daunting list.

Joan knew that border collies met all of her criteria, but she also knew they would be too interested in trying to herd things, including people, so she started looking for a puppy that was mixed breed—part border collie and part other breeds.

At her local Humane Society, she found a little puppy that was just that—part border collie and part akita (a guard dog breed of Japanese origin). Interested, she agreed to foster the puppy for four months. Not surprisingly, it did not take that long for Joan to become clear that the puppy, now named Frankie, was all the things she wanted in a service dog.

Excited to start the journey with her new narcolepsy assistance dog and even though she had found no information about narcolepsy assistance dogs or how to train them, there was information available about how to train an emotional support dog, so that's what Joan set about doing— training Frankie to be an emotional support dog. She hoped an emotional support dog would somehow help her navigate her narcolepsy.

It was Frankie (did she somehow know her destiny?) who took the emotional support dog training a step further. It seemed natural to her to interrupt Joan when Joan got stressed or when a narcolepsy episode seemed close. Frankie just knew when things were not right, and she would nudge and lick Joan until she did something to calm Frankie's concern. How do dogs know? Partly smell, we know, for sure. Narcolepsy, epilepsy, low blood sugar—they all trigger or are triggered by chemical changes in the body, which also cause the body to smell differently. Dogs recognize those chemical changes and become concerned for their loved ones. Perhaps dogs' hyper-vigilance has something to do with it as well, but many people also claim dogs are intuitive.

Joan spoke of a friend of hers who raised sheep. Drinking her early morning coffee and considering the day ahead, the friend decided this would be the day to move the sheep to a different pasture. She got up to put her coffee cup in the sink and glanced out the window at the sheep. She was stunned to see her dog, a border collie, already herding the sheep in the direction of the new pasture, the pasture she had only thought about moving the sheep into, yet she had made no move in that direction. The dog had not been in the kitchen with her, not even in the house, yet there she was, out herding sheep toward the new pasture. That is one example of how amazingly intuitive dogs can be. They seem to read our minds!

Here is another example of an amazing dog. Joan regularly takes Frankie to a local dog park, where she will remove Frankie's harness, so she can be off duty and run and play with the other dogs. Just like people, working dogs need a break from time to time. Joan often sees a man at the dog park who also has an assistance dog. The man and dog walk calmly into the park. The man sits on a bench and removes the assistance dog vest, to signify to the dog that he is no longer on duty, and zoom! Off he speeds to romp and play. Joan knows the man is a combat veteran with post-traumatic stress disorder. Joan saw the man talking on his phone, when suddenly he seemed to shrink into himself. In a flash, and from the far end of the dog park, his dog was at his side, nudging and licking him—saving him. Smell, hyper-vigilance, intuition—all possible explanations for how the dog knew when it was needed.

Assistance dogs are astonishing in their ability to be connected to and be responsive to the humans they care for, and even to humans they are not officially caring for. Joan co-owns a gift shop and alternative healing center where Frankie is always with her. She noticed that Frankie would go to certain customers, sit next to them, and lean into them. Frankie stayed close to them until something let her know it was okay to leave them. Later, when Joan talked to those people, she learned that they were all grieving and were grateful for Frankie's attention. Although surprising and unexpected, Frankie's caring intervention lifted their grief for a little while.

At only two years old, Frankie is already an accomplished assistance dog. Many assistance dogs do not even start their assistance dog training until they are two years old. Most of Frankie's training has consisted of Joan rewarding and encouraging behaviors Frankie does naturally. Her training is ongoing, and she is getting better and better. Joan says that by the time she is four years old, she will be truly incredible.

The Americans with Disabilities Act regulations say a service dog must be under the handler's control at all times and be housebroken.[1] Frankie already meets those requirements, with one exception. She is distracted by children. Joan says that is her fault because when Frankie was a puppy, Joan let her play with children whenever she could. Frankie enjoyed it so much! Now though, Joan has to correct that early learning and train Frankie only to be interested in children when she is not wearing her assistance dog harness. Truly, training never ends.

Joan will be retiring soon and she has been wondering how she will occupy herself then. "Woodworking perhaps?" She chuckles. Actually what she started thinking about is doing something in the area of assistance dogs for narcolepsy—maybe train them herself? Maybe coach other people who want a narcolepsy assistance dog? She is pondering the possibilities. She knows from her own experience how much having an assistance dog can change a person's life. She would like to help other people with narcolepsy improve the quality of their lives the way hers has been improved through her partnership with Frankie.

By the way, Joan remains a safe and licensed driver, thanks largely to Frankie.

References

1. "Service Animals," United States Department of Justice, accessed May 6, 2022, https://www.ada.gov/service_animals_2010.htm

Chapter 19

TERRIE and WILLOW

(Terrie and Willow, photo courtesy of Terrie)

"Where there is a Will[ow] there is a way."

Willow came from a long line of hunting dogs, yet the indications of assistance dog ability were present generations ago. Terrie and her husband, Jerry, owned Willow's great-great-grand-mother, who dutifully walked the children to and from the bus stop (half a mile) every day, persisting even as they became teenagers. Willow's mother was the guardian of all the hobby farm fowl—chickens, ducks, and a para-keet! They were all safe in her presence.

When Willow's mom had a litter of puppies, Terrie and Jerry kept several of them to be hunting dogs. Terrie has Multiple Sclerosis (MS), which was getting worse, and she needed help with daily activities, so Rocky, the larger male, was soon designated to be her Mobility Assist Dog. Life, though, had other plans. Terri has written a story about those events from Willow's point of view, a story that was previously published in Partner in Action[1] and UFFDA[2] periodicals. With Terrie's permission, here is Willow's story.

Willow (photo courtesy of Terrie)

A Hunter Wanna Be!

By Willow … (with help from Mom—Terrie …)

I was born to hunt. My fur Dad, Timber's Gitchee Gummi Hunter, MH (Master Hunter), is a national field champion. When I grew up, I wanted to be a hunter just like him. As a puppy I followed my older brother, Rocky's, example of pointing at critters in the brush; catching them (except for toads—they tasted awful), shaking them until the squeaky stopped, then bringing them back to my human Mom, Terrie. What I didn't understand is why she always threw my gifts to her in the garbage can. Rocky taught me how to catch dragon flies in mid-air, but try as hard as I might I never could catch a bird in mid-air like him. Because birds didn't have squeakers, he would bring them unharmed to Mom and she would just let them fly away.

With the help of Can Do Canines, a service dog training organization, Mom, who has Multiple Sclerosis (MS), was training Rocky to be her mobility assistance dog. I was a sponge listening to Mom as she taught Rocky how to open and shut doors, get her medicine out of the fridge; help take her coat, shoes and socks off; pick up and retrieve anything—even a credit card; and deliver her clunky crutches, even through narrow corridors. I was in awe of his talent.

Rocky (photo courtesy of Terrie)

November 24, 2007, I was six months old and I will never forget that day, it changed my life forever. I watched Rocky jump our four foot backyard fence, chasing down a rabbit to present to Mom. Her ran into a thicket on the neighbor's property, then I heard a single gunshot followed by Rocky's pain filled yipes. A pause, then one more shot, followed by three more quick shots. Then silence. Mom screamed: "No-o-o-o!" The property owner denied any knowledge of the event, even after the local sheriff got involved. I waited by the fence for days, mom cried, I even tried howling for him, but we never saw Rocky again.

Grieving, Mom's MS took a turn for the worse; she couldn't walk, talk very legibly or see clearly. She obviously couldn't keep up with a rambunctious six month old pup like me, so I got sent to boot camp at a hunting school, On Line Retrievers, in Ogilvie, MN. There I fine-tuned my hunting and retrieving skills with birds I could actually catch! I had great fun doing what I was bred to do, I knew I was definitely a Hunter Wanna Be!

After a few months of boot camp I got to go home. Mom was better but her MS didn't go away. In my heart I knew I wanted to help Mom just like Rocky. I surprised her one day when I brought her the clunky crutches when she was having trouble walking. Mom was amazed because she didn't teach me that, but I learned from the best, Rocky! It didn't take long for Mom to realize that I, Willow (the runt of the litter with an extra set of batteries—according to my vet), could be her new mobility assistance dog. After examining my temperament Can Do Canines accepted me into their training program. For a couple years I learned new social skills like going in an airplane and scrunching under the seat, manners with other dogs, ignoring surprising noises, and of course, special skills like getting the fridge meds. It was time for my final evaluation, and Can Do Canines came to our home to film my progress. They asked if I could get an emergency phone (a cordless phone mounted just above the floor) and bring it to Mom anywhere in the house if she fell. We hadn't heard of that skill before! Can Do Canines said they would give us six weeks to learn the skill and then come back to complete the eval and accept me for graduation if I could perform the task.

It was time to put my "extra set of batteries" to work with my great hunting and retrieving skills. While most dogs would be able to make the six-week deadline, I didn't. As soon as Can Do Canines headed down the driveway, Mom got to work; and three hours later me and my batteries were delivering her that phone anytime she asked! We called Can Do Canines and they came out the next day and filmed me, and I was pronounced ready for graduation.

I'm almost fourteen human years-old now and Rocky continues to visit me in my dreams. Especially on

November 24. Mom has told me many times she watches my paws twitch like running and my tail wags away as I sleep on the ottoman in our living room on that day. I do love being Mom's service dog, helping her out and about, and comforting her when she is in the hospital; but deep down, Rocky and I both know I will always be a Hunter Wanna Be!

Epilogue: The original article was transcribed in December of 2020. Wanna know a secret? My given name was Spirit Mountain! When my littermates and I were born Mom decided to name us sequentially based on landmarks along the journey from our home... in the Twin Cities to Duluth where my puppy parents got together. I was the last of the crew, hence "Spirit Mountain," as I mentioned I was also the runt. Earlier Mom had named my older sister "Willow River." Sadly, in just a few hours Willow crossed over the Rainbow Bridge. Since she was now a real spirit our names were switched. However with my "extra set of batteries" many folks thought my name should still have been Spirit. As of May 17, 2021 I can announce with great sorrow and great joy that I am a spirit, and finally a hunter, working the Fields of Heaven in unison with Rocky! Just like Rocky visited after he passed, I visit, too—only much LOUDER! The other day I surprised Mom and Dad (Jerry) by setting off all five of our fire alarms simultaneously! No fire, no smoke, not even a burnt piece of toast, just a reminder that I still have an extra set of batteries!

Photo courtesy of Terrie

When Willow passed away on May 17, 2021, Terrie said it felt like "the cord being ripped from my center." Terrie reports that she and Jerry still sometimes hear Willow's nails clicking on the floor or hear her snores from the living room ottoman. Yes, those assistance dog bonds are strong.

Author's Note: I am sad to say Willow passed away before I could meet with her and Terrie, but after reading

Willow's story, I feel as if I did get to know her at least a little. Terrie is waiting for her grief to subside before she applies for another assistance dog.

References

1. Terrie Schrank, "Hunter Wanna Be!" *Partner in Action* (34), 2021.
2. Terrie Schrank, "Hunter Wanna Be!" UFFDA Chronicles: *The Official Publication of the United Foundation for Disabled Archers 18*(3), Summer 2021.

Acknowledgments

Without the assistance dog teams herein, there would be no book, so thank you so very much, teams, for sharing your information and your experiences so openly with me through the interviews and photo sessions. It has been such a privilege to get to know all of you. My hope is that this book makes a difference for all of you and that the readers enjoy meeting you as much as I did.

A huge thank you to Jett Sophia, lifelong friend and writer extraordinaire, who magically transformed the interviews into beautiful stories. It has been a pleasure to work with you, as always!

To my Women of Words (WOW) writer's group—Ann, Sarah, Linda, Barb, Chris, and Deb—your support, inspiration, and feedback were invaluable. I would not have started—much less finished—the book without all of you.

Thanks to Barb Kellogg, of Barb Kellogg Photography, for showing me the possibilities with her photo essay book about mental illness, *If You Only Knew*[1], and for sharing her photography expertise.

Many thanks to Cahlean Klenke, of About a Dog Photography, for the hours she patiently spent trying to teach me a few things on Adobe Photoshop. Cahlean also has an inspirational book: *Dogs of Minneapolis*[2]. She took some awesome pictures of my oldest dog before he passed away.

Thanks go to another photographer, mentor, and role model, Kathleen Riley of Riley Photography, for beautifully photographing my dogs for her own book, yet to be published: *Senior Souls*. As a mentor, she gave me the courage to move forward and believe in myself and this book.

To my one and only photography course instructor, Peter Happel Christian, thank you for allowing a senior citizen into your class, which greatly increased my confidence as a photographer and introduced me to Photoshop.

Thank you to Alan Peters (director, retired) of Can Do Canines[3] (assistance dog organization) for taking the time to answer, and ask, a multitude of questions and for being so welcoming. Your guidance was pivotal for the direction of the book.

Thank you to the director of Can Do Canines, Jeff Johnson, for continuing to support my contact with Can Do Canines.

With five types of assistance dogs trained at Can Do Canines and over 800 teams graduated, Laurie Carlson of Can Do Canines was instrumental in helping the teams connect with me.

Caren Hansen at Can Do Canines also generously provided permission for their tee shirts, dog capes, and assistance dog Yasmin to appear in the book.

I cannot thank enough my always-positive publisher, Ann Aubitz of Kirk House Publishers, who made everything fun and easy even though I am not easy to work with!

To my neighbors who are so much more than neighbors, who have always been my cheering section and who have listened without judgment to all my ideas, trials, and tribulations, thank you Joanne Clepper, Richard Torrence, and Marilyn Mohr.

Thanks also to my friend Connie Kollmann, who helped me stay sane during COVID lockdown with some horse and country getaways, who has been a source of ongoing support, and who was also a beta reader.

This book has been funded in part through a grant from the Central Minnesota Arts Board, thanks to funds provided by the McKnight Foundation.

References

1. Barb Kellogg, *If You Only Knew* (Burnsville: Fuzion Press, 2019).
2. Cahlean Klenke, *Dogs of Minneapolis* (Unknown: Ingram Spark, 2019).
3. Can Do Canine Assistance Dogs https://candocanines.org

Resources

Assistance Dogs International (ADI)
https://assistancedogsinternational.org
International database of accredited assistance dog training programs listed by country and state.

Can Do Canines Assistance Dogs
9440 Science Center Drive, New Hope, Minnesota 55428
Phone: 763-331-3000
Email: info@can-do-canines.org
Website: www.can-do-canines.org
An ADI-accredited organization providing five types of assistance dogs: mobility, autism, hearing, seizure, and diabetes.

Helping Paws, Incorporated
P.O. Box 634, Hopkins, MN 55343
Phone: (952) 988-9359

Email: info@helpingpaws.org

Website: https://www.helpingpaws.org/

An ADI-accredited organization providing assistance dogs for people with physical disabilities and veterans/first responders with post-traumatic stress disorder.

International Association of Assistance Dog Partners

Website: https://iaadp.org

A nonprofit, cross-disability organization representing people partnered with guide, hearing, and service dogs. Partner Members must attest that their assistance dog meets or exceeds IAADPs Minimum Training Standards. IAADP does not train or certify assistance dogs.

International Guide Dog Federation

Website: https://www.igdf.org.uk/

Leader Dogs for the Blind

1039 South Rochester Road, Rochester Hills, Michigan 48307- 3115

Phone: 248-651-9011 / Toll Free: 888-777-5332

Website: https://www.leaderdog.org

An ADI-accredited organization providing guide dogs for people with blindness.

The Seeing Eye
P.O. Box 375, Morristown, New Jersey 07963-0375
Phone: 973-539-4425
Email: info@seeingeye.org
Website: https://www.seeingeye.org
An ADI-accredited organization providing guide dogs for people with blindness.

United States Department of Veterans Affairs
Website: https://www.prosthetics.va.gov/service-andguidedogs.asp

United States Department of Veterans Affairs
Website: https://www.va.gov/opa/pressrel/pressrelease.cfm?id=2809
Provides service dog benefits to Veterans with mental health disorders

Resources - Humans

This is only a small sample of the resources available. This is not a substitute for medical information or treatment. If you have a medical condition, consult your medical professional for information, treatment, and resources.

American Diabetes Association
Website: https://www.diabetes.org/
National organization funds research, provides information, and delivers services to individuals with all types of diabetes.

The ARC, MN
Website: https://arcminnesota.org
Provides advocacy and resources for people with developmental disabilities.

Deaf and Hard of Hearing Services, State of Minnesota Department of Human Services

Website: https://mn.gov/deaf-hard-of-hearing/

Epilepsy Foundation (national)

Website: https://www.epilepsy.com
Both the national and the local Epilepsy Foundation offer information and support to individuals with epilepsy or seizures and their families.

Epilepsy Foundation of Minnesota

1600 University Avenue West, Suite 300
Saint Paul, MN 55104
Phone: 651.287.2338/800.779.0777
Email: customerservice@efmn.org
Website: https://www.epilepsyfoundationmn.org

Hearing Loss Association of America (Formerly Self Help for Hard of Hearing)

Website: https://www.hearingloss.org/about-hlaa/

Minnesota Autism Center (MAC)

Phone: (952) 767-4200
Website: https://www.mnautism.org
Offers therapeutic services to children ages eighteen months to twenty-one years with autism spectrum disorder (ASD).

National Multiple Sclerosis Society

Website: https://www.nationalmssociety.org

(Minnesota) State Services for the Blind

2200 University Avenue West, Suite 240

Saint Paul, Minnesota 55114

Phone: 651-539-2300

Website: https://mn.gov/deed/ssb

An organization committed to assisting all ages of people in Minnesota with vision loss to achieve independence and their goals. In most cases, there is no cost to consumers.

United Cerebral Palsy

Website: https://www.ucp.org/